CROSSINGS

RICHARD A. HECKLER, Ph.D.

CROSSINGS

*Everyday People, Unexpected Events,
and Life-Affirming Change*

HARCOURT BRACE & COMPANY

New York   San Diego   London

Requests for permission to make copies of any part of the work should
be mailed to: Permissions Department, Harcourt Brace & Company,
6277 Sea Harbor Drive, Orlando, Florida 32887-6777.

Library of Congress Cataloging-in-Publication Data
Heckler, Richard A.
Crossings: everyday people, unexpected events, and life-affirming change/
Richard A. Heckler.—1st ed.
p.   cm.
Includes bibliographical references and index.
ISBN 0-15-100341-6
1. Life change events—Psychological aspects.   2. Life change
events—Psychological aspects—Case studies.   3. Change (Psychology)
4. Spiritual life.   I. Title.
BF637.L53H43   1998
155.9—dc21   97-35165

Text set in Perpetua
Designed by Camilla Filancia
Printed in the United States of America

First edition   A B C D E

For SAMUEL:

The great and unexpected delight of my life.

"The decisive question for man is: Is he related to the infinite or not? That is the telling question of his life. Only if we know that the thing which truly matters is the infinite can we avoid fixing our interests upon futilities and upon all kinds of goals which are not of real importance."

—CARL JUNG

CONTENTS

PROLOGUE

"Ask him about the stone." A few minutes would go by and then the voice again, even, but insistent: "Ask him about the stone." It was the dead of winter in New England. The air was damp and the cold penetrated even the thick stone walls of the old school that was now a community mental health center. Still in my twenties, I was an intern—learning the practice of psychotherapy, by doing. A boon to an already overtaxed and underfunded mental health system, interns—working for free—would be assigned a number of patients and would then receive guidance from seasoned professionals in exchange.

The light was rapidly fading on this February afternoon, and I was sitting opposite a young man, also in his twenties, who was diagnosed as schizophrenic. Dan was prone to episodic flights of ideas, loosely connected and obscure in their meaning; to delusions of reference, in which events, objects, or even people are attributed with unusual and highly idiosyncratic significance; and to auditory and visual hallucinations. Although an amiable sort, Dan spent his days mostly alone. Unable to hold a job, he would shuffle from one end of town to the other, his relationships confined to simple "hi's" and the purchasing of coffee.

This was only our third session, and already I was succumbing to the symptoms that therapists often experience when confused and overmatched. I was becoming sleepy, fidgety, anxious, and, worst of all, I was stealing furtive glances at the clock, though scarcely fifteen minutes had gone by. My patient, on the other hand, was in fine spirits and more than happy to chatter on, uttering a concatenation of sentences that bore little relation to each other—tangential and often nonsensical. Clearly, I was the one suffering more.

Still a neophyte in my chosen craft, I strained to recall theories that would shed light on my predicament. I struggled to create a response that, like Ariadne's thread, could guide me out of the tangled labyrinth of words and ideas in which I was becoming enmired. But mental clarity was not forthcoming, and there seemed to be no application of technique that could help. There was only the occasional prompt from inside. In a voice markedly different than my own—older, seemingly kinder, and wiser—it bid me again: "Ask him about the stone."

This had happened during our first two sessions as well. After each, I reported every detail I could remember to my supervisor, Howard—a man of greater clinical experience and general good humor. But Howard was quite traditional in his training, and during our meeting, when—with some trepidation—I mentioned this message, received from an unknown source, it was clear from the dubious and concerned expression on his face that something was wrong. He admonished that my experience should never be spoken of in the therapeutic interview and deemed that this was the end of it. After I brought it up again during our second meeting, neither one of us was entirely sure that I wasn't becoming psychotic as well, as if schizophrenia were a contagion now invading my mind, too.

The sessions with my supervisor left me just as disquieted as did the hours with my patient, and, feeling without resources within the clinic, I turned to the literature. There I found a wealth of references: voices, visions, fantasies, and hallucinations. But to my dismay, all of these concerned the patient. Probing the psychoanalytic literature, from the many journals to the enormous texts on clinical practice, I found nothing. There simply was no mention of how to proceed if it was the *therapist* who seemed to be hearing voices.

I approached our next appointment with an apprehension that markedly resembled dread. In the days before, I was irritable and easily distracted. A noticeable rift had formed between my supervisor and me. I *was* distressed, but I knew I wasn't crazy (although it seemed that if my tension continued much longer, I might become so). Further, the caution to disregard this kind and intimate voice, to judge it ancillary or even destructive, seemed a kind of violence to myself—some sort of psychic mutilation. I hadn't decided quite what to do, but I did resolve not to allow yet another session to transpire with my feeling hapless and without direction. I vowed to confront Dan's tangential rhetoric, to force him to speak rationally and clearly about his life and predicament. I would wrestle him back to reality, however ungracefully.

The afternoon was clear and bright for our fourth session. The air was icy and dry, and the static electricity common during the winter months had become so charged that the simple act of reaching for a doorknob, or shaking someone's hand, generated a strong shock, startling to the system. I remember the hairs of my arm and head standing on end, as if antennae, searching for signals.

To my astonishment, Dan bounced into my office wearing a T-shirt and a tattered pair of jeans, replete with knee holes. He didn't seem the least bit cold, and he began chattering away almost before sitting down. He was happy and talkative, seeming fairly content to ramble on the entire hour. I could feel my spirits begin to sink.

"Ask him about the stone." The voice unnerved me, entering my consciousness, unbidden and autonomous. I felt rattled, and the thin therapeutic strategy that I devised suddenly seemed pathetic and useless. One cannot confront schizophrenia and expect someone to suddenly toe the line, join the ranks of the sane, and throw away their symptoms like an old coat. Schizophrenia is a deeply debilitating disease of the mind, caused or at least perpetuated by biochemical imbalances within the brain, and reinforced through the profound social isolation it generates. Besides, I had to admit to myself that I hadn't a clue how to lead him from this darkness. The truth was I could barely understand him, and he was much more accomplished at being who he was than was I at being a therapist. "Ask him about the stone." The tone never varied. The voice, always kind and with infinite patience, simply reiterated the command. That, even more than the repetition of the message, proved irresistible.

Dan babbled on, oblivious of the drama unfolding within me; unaware that I had been holding my breath for quite some time; unaware I was sweating, in the middle of winter. I exhaled slowly and looked at him, feigning a confidence I did not feel. Calmly, as if it was common parlance, I interrupted him midsentence and said, "Dan, tell me about the stone."

Without hesitation, he reached into his pocket and removed a small white stone, smooth and nondescript, the kind you would easily find at the seashore. But then he looked at me, really looked at me, and it seemed like it was the first time our eyes truly met—he taking in me, and me him. His agitation ceased. He was simply present. Then he smiled and said, "This is the stone that Jesus gave me. I take it with me everywhere I go."

We sat in silence for some time. Dan had shared something fundamental and precious. Although its veracity could be contested, that stone represented proof of his own significance, of a sense of connection and belonging he could count on within the swirling confusion, rejection, and alienation of his disease. In those few moments, there was no therapist, and there was no patient. Just two young men, charting their ways, each with his own set of amulets and beliefs, meeting at a crossroads.

Dan's diagnosis suddenly seemed immaterial to me. To my perception, he was perfect just as he was. I felt love for Dan in that silence. I could admire the strength of his character and the resilience of his spirit despite crushing odds. I didn't need him to be any different.

Perhaps it's self-serving, but I remember very little of what transpired for the rest of that hour . . . or in the weeks that followed. I would like to claim that Dan was "cured" in those moments or that he made marked improvements thereafter—that he left our session clearheaded and sane. I'd like to believe that he felt moved, as I did, by the simple power of our unconditional presence and regard for one another. After years of negotiating the state's mental health system and the prejudice that accompanies mental illness, it could be possible.

It is more probable, however, that the greater impact was experienced by this young therapist. Desperate and without the necessary clinical experience, I finally surrendered to the voice inside. Although I may not have discovered a cure for schizophrenia, I did discover something essential for a therapist (and perhaps all of us) to know: that there exists levels of information and guidance that lay beneath consensual reality. If we are willing to take a leap, and suspend the doubt that often accompanies stepping outside the bounds of convention, we may find ourselves on a path or in terrain quite beyond what we ever thought possible.

It's not scientific in the traditional sense—I cannot replicate the experience or find an explanation that conforms to the laws of parsimony, but something undeniably profound did happen that afternoon. Ultimately, people are not problems to be solved, but experiences waiting to happen. That voice waited patiently, until one stubborn young intern was finally ready to listen.

CROSSINGS

INTRODUCTION

"We must assume our existence as broadly as we in any way can; every-thing, even the unheard of must be possible in it. This is at bottom the only courage that is demanded of us: to have courage for the most strange, the most inexplicable."

—RAINER MARIA RILKE

"O Ship of Zion"

Karl worked as an enforcer for organized crime. He had spent much of his adult life drug-addicted, buying and dealing large quantities of cocaine and heroin. By the age of thirty-five, he had matured into a fearsome sociopath—cold and violent. Wherever he went, Karl carried both knives and handguns. In restaurants and bars, he had learned to sit with his back to the wall. Though it was a miracle just to extricate himself from such a life,[1] that miracle was followed by another. Karl had successfully eluded the FBI for months, but finally, he was ap-prehended. To his surprise, he was offered a choice between jail and rehabilitation. He submitted to a religiously based detox program, one approved by the court. Each Wednesday night, members of the program would appear before the church and tell their stories. Within a month, Karl was called upon to testify in front of the congregation. Tone-deaf throughout his life and absent of musical ability, he nevertheless prepared himself, with the help of the pastor, to sing the old spiritual, "O Ship of Zion." Karl walked to the center of the stage. His knees were shaking and his breath was quick. He pondered the absurdity of being so nervous, after a life of such unemotional, calculated brutality. And he waited like a choirboy for his cue.

To his astonishment, Karl hit every note. His pitch was perfect and his voice was full and rich with vibrato. Karl felt a majesty he had never before known, and as he exited the stage, a deep peace and wholeness surrounded him. It was then he distinctly heard a voice, even and kind, and clearly not his own.

> I heard [his] voice whispering, "Now this is why I saved you all those times. I had a calling for you here. I want you to tell people that no matter how bad things are, there's hope. I want you to tell them that."

Karl had avoided church his whole life, but he was certain it was Jesus who spoke to him. The power of those moments, and the meaning he ascribed to them, determined the trajectory of Karl's rehabilitation. Later that evening, he became convinced of his purpose and his calling. He kicked both alcohol and drugs in one night, never to let them return. Clean and sober for many years now, he has become a gentle and insightful man. Karl works as a minister to the inner-city homeless, and, in his spare time, he sings in a rock 'n' roll band.

Sooner or later it happens to us all. Something or someone comes hurtling through the trance of our everyday lives and startles us. It may be a sudden promotion or a birth of twins, the diagnosis of terminal illness or the death of a loved one. Sometimes the unexpected arrives in a dramatic form: A woman hears a voice, its message speaking directly to a present dilemma, but there is no one around. Someone takes a walk in the country, and a religious figure appears to him offering direction for the future. A man is about to step off a curb but feels a hand pulling him back as a truck barrels through the intersection. His heart racing, he looks around but finds no one. A woman is pronounced medically dead, but consciousness continues, and she experiences a warmth or a light or an almost inexpressible feeling of love and caring. A kind but firm voice instructs her to return to life in order to complete various tasks or confront certain difficulties.

Most often, the form of the unexpected is subtle—a curious exchange with a stranger on the subway; knowing that we will run into an old friend, though we haven't spoken in years; we suddenly spy an advertisement on a billboard that seems to speak directly to us, or overhear a conversation that is identical in its content to what we were pondering at that very moment.

Events such as these are powerful and they can change lives. Most often, however, we pause only briefly. Our walk momentarily slows as we fashion possible explanations. Most of us lack a worldview broad enough to explain what has transpired, however, and we disregard it. Rarely, amid the pace of our lives, do we take the time to go back and truly investigate what has occurred. Many have had destiny cross their paths—and didn't know what to do about it.

But what if we consider these events to be signals or messages? What if we attempt to intuit a meaning to the unexpected, or at least acknowledge that something significant has occurred beyond what we ever believed possible? The stories that follow show that when people do so, they cross into a profound and mysterious territory. If they can tolerate its strangeness and the inevitable sense of dislocation it engenders, the experience can yield profound treasures—deeper insight, a clearer sense of purpose, and a greater understanding of the world and their place in it.

Not everyone who experiences the extraordinary chooses to follow its lead. The event is dismissed, and the call is denied.[2] But those who consider its meaning embark on an epic journey, a pilgrimage that has been chronicled throughout the ages in our myths and tales—the journey of self-discovery and spiritual understanding. According to theologians, mythologists, and psychologists, this is the most important journey of our lives.

Crossings is a book for people who have experienced the unexpected and followed its call, for people puzzled about experiences they've had, and for those who are interested to learn about the mysterious borderland where the psychological world ends and the enigmatic world of the spirit begins. Those interviewed in this book are ordinary people who have had extraordinary experiences. But there are, in fact, many for whom this is true. In *Crossings,* the people who speak to us have all responded to the unexpected in a particular way—by wrestling with its meaning and making unconventional choices—and that has led them down a road less traveled and into a future that they never thought possible.

Crossings is a book about lives transformed by the unexpected, but it is not an accounting of the occult, or a protracted discussion about the nature of the unusual, or even a treatise concerning whether, in fact, supernatural phenomena actually exist. At this time, such a discussion seems to me to be effort unwisely spent. Helpers in the latter part of this century— physicians, psychotherapists, and clergy alike—have listened as their patients, clients, and parishioners told stories of radically unusual experiences. They were most often unbidden and incurred dramatic effects. Similar tales have emerged throughout the country (and the world) and cross the demographic categories of race and ethnicity, class, profession, religion, age, and sexual preference. In fact, unless one believes there is a nationwide conspiracy afoot to challenge the fundamental underpinnings of the Cartesian-based scientific paradigm, one cannot marvel at the persistence of such stories, the unblemished sanity of many of those relating them, and the commonalties that lay beneath the individual differences in circumstance (despite the fact that, most often, the subjects of these events have little or no exposure to unusual phenomena, or to chronicles of similar events by others).

Rather, A New Psychology of the Unexpected attempts to articulate just how change happens when people are spurred by the unexpected. In each case, those from whom we will hear experienced something that fell far beyond their sense of the possible and far beyond conventional notions of science and psychology. In responding to that event, not as an inexplicable anomaly, but as a communication not yet understood, the people in these pages powerfully changed their lives. Inspiration replaced despair, renewed spiritual inquiry replaced the quagmire of addiction, and each found him- or herself making personal changes that from the outside may have seemed impractical, impulsive, even foolhardy, but from the inside, were perfectly right.

I began my research for *Crossings* by studying the literature, in this case concerning unusual and extraordinary events. I perused accounts of psychological, parapsychological, and spiritual experiences of many kinds, but as I continued to explore, I became puzzled. It seemed an important dynamic was consistently absent in the analyses of these studies. Did an unexpected event, just by the fact that it occurred, change someone's life? Was its transformational power solely derived from its inexplicable oddness, or was there a part that the person him- or herself had to play? As I read hundreds of accounts, I began to entertain some opinions. It seemed that the event itself represented the passive component of change—someone suddenly discovers that something quite unusual is happening. All that is called for at that moment is to watch, and let the moment play itself out with as little interference as possible. But what did people *do* with these events? How did they make sense of them? What choices did they make based on them? Wasn't there also an active component—a nascent sense of meaning ascribed to the event, a decision silently taken, a response made? And if so, what was the dynamic relationship between the passive and active dimensions of this adventure, such that, combined, its transformative power could fundamentally alter the course of a life?

Armed with these questions, I began my research in earnest, traveling throughout the country, speaking to people in person. I was invited into their homes and offices, or in makeshift spaces—coffeehouses or a favorite park. There, people spoke about experiences that transformed their lives. Often the chronicle began haltingly, for I was a stranger and people had learned to guard the details for fear of misunderstanding and quick judgment. Over time, I learned to speak to this directly, and by doing so, trust was cultivated and we laid the foundation for the unraveling of candid and compelling tales.

My request was a simple one: "Please tell me about your

life before the event; about the event itself, in as much detail as you can; and about what happened within you and in your life as a result." What ensued were hours spent together, recounting each episode and reflecting upon their deepest significance.

This type of research defies neat categorization. It violates a central tenet of classical scientific inquiry. Social and physical scientists are taught that the scientific method, with its fidelity to parsimony, quantifiability, and repeatability, provides the standard to which all legitimate research must conform. It is a methodology, inspired by Sir Isaac Newton, developed by René Descartes, and refined throughout the last four centuries. Although the bounty reaped through its discipline is vast, and touches nearly every facet of our lives, many of us have now observed a critical deficit—the Cartesian method also subtly limits the boundaries of what we consider real. As historians of science in the latter part of the twentieth century have critiqued, what Cartesian science could not examine in the laboratory or quantify on paper was deemed not to exist. Morris Berman discusses this in his provocative treatise, *The Re-enchantment of the World:*

> Construing reality mechanically is, however, a way of participating in the world, but it is a very strange way, because our reality system officially denies that participation [i.e. intuitive, psychic, spiritual experiences] exists. [These experiences] cease to be conscious because we no longer attend to [them] . . . but [they] do not cease to exist.[3]

The Cartesian paradigm was less a rigorous scientific refutation than a religious and political response to the animism of the previous centuries. It was an endeavor to eliminate what was felt to be superstition (disparagingly referred to as "enthusi-asm") and to create one, consensually agreed upon, model of how the world worked.

In truth, no method, no one theory, can encapsulate the infinite variety of human experience. The traditional scientific method has been too universally applied, leaving too many ex-periences ignored and too much compelling data untouched. In our desire to end groundless superstition, we also deny our-selves critical information, road maps about how we negotiate the myriad dips and turns of a life. We become more isolated, and we overtax an already burdened rational intellect in an attempt to comprehend the mystery of our lives.

Whereas traditional science demands that the researcher maintain an objective distance from that which he or she studies, I attempt to get closer.[4] This method of investigation, which I call "participatory research," requires that one attempt to step into the shoes of the other in order to truly comprehend what is being described, at the deepest levels possible. One not only records the story, but the storyteller. Participatory research stands at the interface of a number of disciplines: psychology, anthropology, and sociology. To this, *Crossings* adds another two: spiritual inquiry and oral history. As people come to life on these pages, their very personal stories become universal and we may see ourselves in their reflections.

Within the intricacies of these tales there can be found a few simple ideas. First, there is a dialogue occurring of which we are little aware. Some experience it as a communication from the deepest parts of our selves—a response from the soul concerning our greatest aspirations or a missive from the "small voice within." Others feel a connection with a higher or greater intelligence or power. People become aware of this dialogue, often for the first time, through the entrance of the radically unexpected into their lives, and when they do, they are stopped in their tracks. During these experiences, and during the states of mind and body they engender, everything extraneous falls away and only the heart's greatest desire and one's fundamental sense of purpose are addressed. The stories in *Crossings* show that this dialogue creates an irresistible momentum that propels one into a strange land—filled with magic, fraught with danger, laden with meaning, and potent with a healing capacity.

Second, there is a pattern of personal evolution that guides the journey of our lives. (Regardless of whether or not we are aware of it, we nevertheless stumble and trip our way through this passage.) This pattern is reflected in great myths, legends, fairy tales, and heroic quests throughout the written and oral history of humankind. In *Crossings,* these themes are arranged into a developmental model I call the Stages of Transformation. This model identifies six steps in the pattern of personal change as a result of an encounter with the unexpected. The Stages of Transformation were born from analyzing nearly one hundred hours of interviews, and in that analysis, the Stages emerged as the universal elements and the common threads that wove through the process of each person's encounter with the unexpected:

- The first stage, the Slumber, represents the trance of everyday life, the time before one's world has been shaken by the unexpected. It is a time in which routine concerns overshadow deeper contemplation and the scope of one's life seems more or less confined to the habitual. Some of the lives chronicled here were proceeding evenly, even happily. People were vocationally and financially successful, although from

time to time, questions of life purpose and deeper understanding would nip at the edges of their awareness. Some of
those interviewed led lives filled with pain before the
unexpected—the death of a loved one, a descent into drug
addiction, an incipient divorce, a rape. Symbolized in fables
by a great slumber, the status quo sets the stage for the
unsuspected entry of the fantastic.

- With the Call, the adventure begins. The unexpected arrives
  on the wings of surprise. Whether subtle or dramatic, it stops
  us. Its exotic nature prohibits inattention or denial, and in
  these moments we gain entry into a world of magic and
  meaning previously hidden. The unexpected speaks to each
  of us in a precise language, both intimate and bizarre. It is as
  if a code has been created especially for us, to address our
  deepest questions. Sometimes depicted as a bolt of lightning,
  the unexpected momentarily captures us, and *calls* us to venture into a world in which such things are possible. The unexpected demands that we surrender limiting behaviors and
  beliefs, however cherished, and stretch into a greater life. It
  is possible to view unexpected events as simply isolated in-
  cidents or anomalous curiosities, but in the Stages of Transformation, they are considered the harbingers of nothing less
  than a life quest and the beginning of an extraordinary
  journey.

- The third stage is called Incubation. Highly unusual events
  cleave one's relationship to routine life. Mental, emotional,
  and physical systems have been so impacted that one is hard
  pressed to think, feel, and act as before. After the event,
  people need time to assimilate what has transpired. Withdrawal from social interaction is common and privacy is often

required. Incubation marks the beginning of a necessary period of separation, in which the seeds of the unexpected germinate and one waits for meaning and direction to emerge. The image of the chrysalis is particularly apt here.

- The fourth stage involves the Search for Meaning. Questions abound as people attempt to grapple with the enormity of what has transpired: How could such a thing happen? Why me? Who am I now? Where is my place? These are common responses to the unexpected. In some cases, the meaning of the event seems immediately clear. People report a sense of knowing and a quality of certainty they may never have experienced before. For others, the meaning evolves more slowly. Time may need to pass, and steps may need to be taken. The Search for Meaning reflects a powerful choice made in the wake of the unexpected—that the event contains meaning. This choice, almost as much as the particular meaning, creates an irresistible inner momentum that carries one back into the world.

- In the fifth stage, the Leap, people make decisions based on an emergent sense of meaning. Meaning creation and Incubation seem to engender a force from deep within, and people at this point often feel propelled to act. Decisions are made that often appear unconventional and counterintuitive, even reckless. To the observer, they may appear highly uncharacteristic in comparison to one's normal range of behavior, as if one is jumping from a cliff, but to the person making it, the Leap feels absolutely right and intuitively clear.

- Finally, in the Integration phase, people reenter their lives, changed in substantial and often dramatic ways. In addition to the specific passage they have negotiated, all describe one profound and fundamental transformation in common—having developed a working relationship to the unexpected. The entire experience has expanded one's sense of the possible, and people have crafted ways to recognize, open to, and understand the unexpected—however big or small—as it continues to manifest in their lives. Developing a working relationship to the unexpected yields dramatic benefits. Those interviewed report the following:

- greater flexibility of mind
- greater emotional resilience
- greater willingness to take risks
- clearer sense of life purpose (vision)
- greater sense of acceptance of and peace in the present
- paradoxically, a greater sense of control
- an expanded sense of identity
- a profoundly greater sense of possibility[5]

The awareness of the Stages of Transformation can be of inestimable value. When our lives have taken unexpected turns or when we find ourselves in the inevitable periods of confusion that accompany change, we needn't fear that we have fallen off the flat edge of the earth. Understanding the patterns of personal evolution brings perspective and solace—knowing that we are embarked on a path that people have traveled since the beginning of time. This path has a beginning, a middle, and an end. There is method to its apparent madness, and that method yields patience, perspective, and wholeness.

The people you are about to meet had silently placed a period at the end of the sentence of their lives. Whether they were overtly suffering, or whether life progressed in standard fashion, a decision had been made, consciously or not, that they must remain within the confines of the conventional. A promising young law student agreeably follows the counsel that parents and extended family provide for him, barely aware of the nascent impulse to decide about his own life. His passivity brings him to the edge of military combat. A Native American woman, raised away from her culture and its traditions, leads a life of gambling and alcohol, until the sudden, unexplainable appearance of a visitor. A British physician, heartbroken from the death of his wife, receives an unexpected and life-transforming communication. And a top-secret military intelligence officer experiences a vision that unearths her deeply spiritual leanings.

What happened to Tara, a mother of seven children, or Charlotte, a family psychologist deeply exhausted and fighting for her life, seemed to defy explanation. Before these events transpired, they would never have believed them to be possible, and they certainly never expected to be central protagonists in such an incomprehensible drama. The events that occurred in the lives of those chronicled here were mysterious and compelling, as if an urgent message were being sent from somewhere, in a code both bizarre and intimately familiar. How they chose to decipher those messages determined the direction of the rest of their lives.

Crossings is ultimately a book about people who have crossed a deeply ingrained, scientifically and culturally reinforced boundary, and traveled beyond what is thought to be possible. Often, through no intention or desire of their own, their experiences shook the very foundations of their belief about reality. This is a book about their response to these events—an impassioned desire to discover what had happened to them and what it meant. That desire, to find a context that was big enough to contain their experience, prompted a quest and, unbeknownst to them at first, the beginning of a profound rite of passage.

We have few maps in western culture for the quest for wholeness, and for understanding, and for making meaning of the unexpected when it inserts itself into our lives and bids us to change. *Crossings* is an attempt to create a path where the forest seems especially thick and where the vines threaten to grab and pull us under. *Crossings* extends beyond the reach of simply chronicling the fantastic. Contained within these pages are the watershed experiences and responses to them that emerge from a deep wellspring of inspiration, contemplation, and courage. Life transformation is not for the fainthearted. Even events that seemed immediately healing, full of grace and magic, had to be followed by iconoclastic thinking and bold decision making. *Crossings* is not only about what happens when people experience the unexpected, but how people learn to stop, surrender who they thought they were, and suspend their most precious beliefs. In that act, they discover an inner oracle, an unshakable reservoir of wisdom, insight, and direction. And they learn to listen.

Rebecca

THE NIGHT-SEA JOURNEY

"Unexpected invitations to travel are dancing lessons from God."
—KURT VONNEGUT

Rites of passage are prescribed Night-Sea Journeys; choreographed dark nights of the soul, whose form has been handed down from generation to generation. In indigenous cultures, they were designed to create pivotal somatic, psychological, and spiritual experiences that, in one master stroke, introduced tribal members to the perennial wisdom of their ancestors, proposed a context for current travails, proffered a sense of direction, and then provided the real tools required to get there. Those who survived their ordeals were considered "twice-born"—the first referring to their biological birth, and the second, into a birth of a more elemental connection with life and a deeper understanding of their place in it. In many traditions, it was this life, now invested in and guided by the spirit, that was considered the real one.

The motif of the Night-Sea Journey in myths reflects the recognition that the rite of passage is a form of self-surrender or annihilation. Something in us must die to allow something deeper to emerge.[6] The unexpected sounds a Call, and if we respond, we are propelled (often without map or compass) into the waters of a deep inner journey, one that takes us beneath easy labels and self-identifications. Rites of passage are voyages in which we become swallowed by a storm of powerful emotions, supercharged symbols, hideous and heavenly creatures, and intimations of death on the way to realizing our true nature and sense of purpose.

Rebecca wasn't thinking about rites of passage, or her true nature for that matter, when she signed on as cook for the voyage to the Virgin Islands. She was simply looking for some excitement, and perhaps a bit of romance. Rebecca's story serves well to begin our look at the lives of people who pass through the stages of this mysterious passage. In her tale, one can clearly recognize the stages through which one progresses, from the ubiquitous trance of everyday life, into the Call, and through the difficult, and sometimes terrifying separation that occurs during the Incubation phase. Ultimately, hers is a heroic story of overcoming enormous peril and befriending her fear, all at a relatively young age. That experience, and the meaning gleaned from it, determined the direction of the rest of her life.

The past few years had been difficult ones. The depression of her late adolescence had quietly, almost by stealth, overtaken her again, and her days were occupied either with waitressing at a local diner or in rambling conversation with friends who had stayed in Massachusetts after high school. Rebecca had quit college and spent the next few years traveling around the country, letting herself be drawn to whatever seemed most interesting. She had heard about an educational institute in Colorado, the Naropa Institute, that was developing a reputation as a hotbed for the study of spirituality and poetry. Rebecca enjoyed both the music and mystery of poetry, and it was to verse and meter she turned in an attempt to access something essential, yet still unformed inside her.

The class was a six-week whirlwind. Rebecca was as simultaneously moved and overwhelmed by the personalities as by the course work: the explosive, unself-conscious expressiveness of Allen Ginsberg; Anne Waldman's deep sense of the dramatic moment, even in simple conversation; the mischievous, coyote-like Gary Snyder, who would dance his poetry as much as recite it; and the laconic and stolid William S. Burroughs. There were poetry classes and readings, coupled with meditation instruction, but although the spiritual side seemed interesting, Rebecca found she had little patience for the practice of sitting on a meditation cushion.

I had learned a modicum of Buddhism there, but I wasn't very serious about it. I meditated only once the whole time I was there. I do remember that one distinctly. Feeling a lot of pain, trying to sit still. Coming out of it feeling very spacy and light-headed. It was strange. I enjoyed it, but it was also very painful and although I knew it was remarkable in a way, I wasn't very interested in pursuing it. After that summer, as I was struggling with the depression again, I ignored the practice. I knew that people were getting a lot out of meditation but it still didn't feature prominently for me.

A young adult of more than ample intelligence and creativity, Rebecca most often felt disconsolate and directionless. In some unnameable way, the feeling seemed to afflict her whole family—vacant of inspiration, as if no one believed the future would or could hold anything positive. The melancholy that surrounded her house would alternately drive Rebecca away, even as far as the West Coast, but inevitably, she would find herself pulled back again. Drawn to some event—a course, concert, or gathering—her excitement would soon ebb, unable to sustain her for long.

One day, an old boyfriend called. He had just enrolled in a meditation course and asked if she would meet him when it ended. Rebecca was surprised both that her friend had been interested in meditation and that there was a retreat center only an hour away.

I went to pick him up and got to experience the atmosphere there at the end. It was extremely powerful. People seemed so serene; collected and soft in a welcoming way. They seemed very centered to me. I knew I should go do that. I was thinking, *Why was I ditzing around with my life, struggling with this depression?* I had a glimmer of an idea that I could help myself, and that seemed surprising, too, after years and years of thinking I was helpless. I told the restaurant I was

going on vacation for two weeks. It was a three-month retreat and I was fully intending to quit my job, if the retreat
truly was what I was looking for.

The Insight Meditation Center in Barre is nestled in the
rolling hills and valleys of central Massachusetts. Relatively new,
it is cradled in some of the oldest mountains in North America.
A few years before, two young Americans, Jack Kornfield and
Joseph Goldstein, had returned from prolonged stays in India
and Thailand, where they had become monks.[7] Independently,
each had enrolled in the Peace Corps with the intention to stay
and learn an ancient form of Buddhist meditation practice, vi-
passana, that arose from the Theravadin tradition. Upon their
return, they found many who were interested in the practices,
and encouraged, they began to offer short classes. While its
historical offspring, Zen and Tibetan Buddhism, contained more
ornate ritual, in the prayers, practices, and even clothing worn,
Theravadin practice was relatively spare—its ritual minimal and
instructions easily accessible to westerners. Interest grew rapidly
and soon Jack and Joseph, with the help of their students, purchased a former Catholic seminary and founded a Western retreat site for the Eastern teachings.

> So I did the retreat and found it incredibly profound. I was
> very strict with myself; held to all the rules. Very pious.
> There was a lot of physical pain—my back, neck and
> knees—that I had to learn to surrender to, and there was a
> lot of emotional pain. But toward the middle of the retreat,
> my body felt more relaxed and I was constantly having re-
> alizations about what my psychological patterns were, why I
> felt so depressed, and why my relationships were the way
> they were. I had always been terribly self-conscious and self-
> critical, but by the end of the retreat, much of it seemed to
> have dissolved. I worked through an amazing amount of stuff
> and felt tremendously grateful for the opportunity. When I

returned, I felt fresh and ready for another adventure. That's when I found out about the trip.

It looked stunning. The forty-two-foot slip perched majestically in the water, the sides freshly washed, the wooden deck burnished and waxed, and the sails almost luminescent in the sun. Rebecca, in her role as cook, busied herself with packaging the food and water, creating menus for each day, and learning to store the items correctly in the cabin below. The crew, old friends from high school, seemed experienced enough after having taken the required courses in navigation and sailing.

The plan was to sail to St. John, starting in North Carolina, and hugging the coast until we made a little jump over to the islands. The crew had sailed before, I was clearly the amateur here, so I was relying heavily on their experience. I didn't really think of the dangers involved. I think I was still really attracted to the captain, an ex-lover, and I wanted an adventure. The first glimmer of things not working too well was when I discovered that the captain hadn't given the coast guard a copy of our route. He said he didn't have enough time and he wanted to get going.

So we left in the evening and sailed through the night. It was gorgeous! I remember there was particle algae floating on the water that glittered in the moonlight. There were light, warm winds, and we were sailing beautifully. It was just idyllic. And then, suddenly, everything changed.

It is characteristic of storms at sea to arise quickly, almost instantly catching less experienced sailors by surprise. The warm winds had seduced the young crew, disguising the low-pressure system about to fall around them and cloaking the savagery of what was to come. The blizzard, which had begun to blanket the entire East Coast, would become the biggest and most destructive in a decade.

Thirty-foot waves. They were house-sized! Suddenly the boat seemed very small. We were caught in a blinding storm, freezing rain and snow, and the inexperience of the crew began to show . . . it was pretty extreme. We went from easy sailing to emergency sailing, which meant we had to unfurl the sails, but in our panic, we didn't take them down in time and they shredded. They ripped out and were useless. The captain only brought one set, which is absolutely against the rules, so the only thing we could do then was use the rudder to steer the bow into the waves.

After a few hours of that, we were cold and wet and the captain decided to jerry-rig the tiller and go into the cabin. Within ten minutes, we were hit broadside and rolled over. Everybody was thrown across the cabin. Miraculously, nobody got hurt. I landed in a fetal position in a corner, on top of the stove. The rest of the crew hit the other side pretty hard and for the next couple of hours, total chaos and panic ensued. It was a hell-realm. We had taken on lots of water, up to our knees in the cabin, and we didn't know if there was a hole in the boat. The boat righted itself—the keel has a ton of lead in it—but we had completely turned over. At one point, the mast pointed straight down into the water.

Rebecca began to radio for help while the crew began the furious task of bailing water. A number of ships responded and requested their position, but the captain could provide no information.

It was then I found out that although the captain had been taking navigation courses, they were only for ancient navigation instruments! All he had on board was a sextant and compass, and because we couldn't see the sky—we couldn't even get on deck—they were useless. I heard people on the radio saying to one another, "Did you hear that?" "Sounds like they're really in trouble." "But where are they? Where are they?" It felt like I was at my own funeral. Finally, the radio went dead. The batteries went dead. We had lost all power because everything had been swamped. Then we lost the engine.

The ocean had swallowed them and then spit them back into a different world. Familiar reference points were dissolved. The passage of time could not be measured. Days were uniformly gray in the snow and rain, and the night seemed to stretch out interminably. Their sense of scale had been supplanted as well. The ship, having once appeared so elegant and capable, now seemed lilliputian, a paltry protection against waves the size of mansions. With every ascent onto another enormous wall of water, the members of the crew reflexively held their breath and waited to discover whether once again they would be submerged. With stomachs churning and their throats tight with fear, the crew was repulsed by food. And, cramped together in close quarters, each person withdrew, attempting to find refuge inside themselves.

In shock and growing quickly exhausted, Rebecca climbed into her wet bunk and buried herself in the only book she could find.

> It was Clavell's *Shogun,* and the first part of the book was about a shipwreck! Blow by blow, it was basically what was happening to us. The terror was completely physiological: there was a rush of adrenaline as the boat was tossed and then I'd get real still, trying to feel if we had capsized. We were about 100 miles offshore and I remember trying to conceptualize what a mile of water was 'cause that's how deep I thought we were. I was trying to imagine what it would be like to drown in a mile of water.

Each person was assigned a two-hour shift on deck to guide the boat and prevent being capsized again. The others checked for holes and bailed water. It was a sound idea, but the chronic

stress, coupled with the lack of food and sleep, left them vul-
nerable to dangerous tricks of the mind.

> We were too sick to eat, and after four or five days, everyone
> began having hallucinations. I was out there guiding the tiller.
> You know, I had never done this in my life, but I had to
> take my shift too . . . and I heard these voices out on the
> water calling, "Help! Help!" It was very convincing. It
> sounded just like someone was out there. Another time, one
> of the men who was supposed to be on watch came back
> down into the cabin after just fifteen minutes. We all yelled,
> "What are you doing!" and he replied that his brother had
> come to relieve his watch. But there was no one up there!
> It was dangerous and very strange. Real psychosis.

The unexpected had deposited Rebecca and the crew into
an altered world. Normal perception had eroded and visual and
auditory hallucinations compromised a waning grasp of shared
reality. In a very real sense, Rebecca and the crew had become
invisible.

> There was a kind of story line in the group, that since we
> were in shipping lanes, a ship would come along any minute
> and they would see us and call the coast guard and we'd be
> back on land eating ice cream that night. It was a kind of
> denial, and it was an excuse not to have to do anything.
> "Let's just sit here and they'll find us."

> It seemed reasonable from a certain perspective, but it was
> a very ignorant idea because the truth of it is that big ships
> run over little boats all the time on the high seas. In fact,
> shipping lanes are by far the *most* dangerous place to be.
> Pretty early in our trip, ships passed us. At first we were
> absolutely convinced we were seen and we were waving and
> blowing our horn . . . but the ship would go right by. I don't
> know how many ships we encountered, lots, but sometimes
> we had to actually do everything we could to get *out* of their
> way. They were more of a danger than the waves! Huge

tankers and freighters, computer piloted so that, once they were out at sea, they would not see small ships. They would run them over like ants. At no point did anybody stop and help. None of them seemed to have reported anything to the coast guard either. It was like we didn't exist.

A simple barometer was all the crew had to intuit their fate. Almost hourly, they would check to see if, by some miracle, the atmospheric pressure had begun to rise. Ritualized, after so many repetitions, the crew would leave the warm, if wet, protection of their sleeping bags to check if the tempest was passing, and then attempt to suppress the disappointment and the panic that lay just below that when they discovered the opposite. There were in fact some periods of calm seas, but they would serve only to mask another assault by the storm.

About the fourth day, during a particularly vigorous onslaught of rain and high winds, Rebecca found herself on deck, tending her shift. The storm had replaced another short period of calm, and spirits were sinking with the barometric pressure. It seemed to be the absolute nadir of their voyage. It was then that Rebecca discovered a lifeline.

> I was again thinking about drowning in a mile of water. The thought seemed to possess me. I would feel real deep terror and obsess about it some more and then feel more afraid. At one point, however, I noticed that if I didn't fan the flames of the terror, it didn't continue. If I stopped thinking about it for a moment, it didn't seem to be sustainable by itself. Even though the danger still existed—there were still thirty-foot waves and we still hadn't a clue where we were—I noticed the fear was only a momentary thing. This was really surprising and interesting!

It wasn't tangible in the ordinary sense. No one had arrived in a rescue craft or helicopter. The storm hadn't abated. In fact, it got worse. But in those moments, Rebecca was curiously transported. And she was doubly surprised: first, in her discovery of the impermanence of her terror, and second, that she had, in fact, become interested in anything at all other than her survival.

> I began to find the state of mind I was in during the three-month [meditation] retreat. I started counting my breaths and just staying with that for longer periods of time. I would notice the terror arise—it was still there—but I wasn't getting invested in it, claiming it as myself. I just let it arise in my mind; then I'd examine it rather than be afraid of it. I noticed that the terror was made up of a lot of different emotions, and that they seemed to continually change—fear, then anger, then fatigue, then sadness—and then I'd let it go. I began to think that the fear was mostly just a neurological event that would pop up and there would be all this adrenaline and then it would subside by itself.
>
> Then, there was another surprise. I started to experience a lot of time in between those bouts of terror. There was a spaciousness. There were even moments when I experienced great beauty in the situation, especially when I was on watch. The fury of nature and the power of it all was just arm's length away, and there were increasing periods of time when I felt awe and even reverence for it, but I didn't feel afraid! I mean, the waves continued, solid walls of water bearing down on us and all you could do is steer the boat up them as best you could . . . like sailing up a mountain. And in addition to that, I couldn't quite trust everyone's sanity. All of us, from time to time, were going off the deep end, no pun intended. But, it seemed like a miracle to experience those moments.

It was as if Rebecca had found a trapdoor beneath the water; someplace quiet, still, and free of the nightmare. And as she continued her practice, she noticed two things. First, she was becoming calmer and more self-possessed, even during periods of great danger. Second, she realized that, if they had any chance to survive whatsoever, she would have to be the one to gather the frazzled crew and coordinate them. Rebecca had always been more comfortable either alone or couched in the background, following along with the group. By the fifth day at sea, however, and with no apparent help in sight, she found a sense of command she had never known.

> I had been very timid, even subservient, up until that point, especially in relation to the captain. But I ended up being active in a way that was very uncharacteristic for me. Nobody had eaten anything in five days and everyone was having more hallucinations. One guy was punching the walls in fear and anger while the captain was lamenting about never being able to see his kids again. Meanwhile, I was getting more collected, monitoring my thoughts and my breath. Everyone was at their worst, and these guys, they were real macho at first, were now completely raw.

> So I called a meeting and said, "I don't care if you throw up. We're all gonna start eating again." They looked sicker just at the suggestion! Then I said, "And stop imagining that someone's gonna save us. We have to realize that this is our home for now and we have to start living normally and we have to start taking care of ourselves." And I told them we had to sew the sails.

The crew accepted their new leader, as hers was the only rational voice to emerge from the madness. Compliant, they began to eat, and a bit more lucid, they crafted a plan to sail due west. They were approximately 100 miles from shore, so if the captain's ancient instruments were adequate to the task, and if they were skillful and lucky enough to survive, they'd reach landfall in three days. Every evening, through snow and freezing rain, their eyes turned west in hopes of seeing lights, landfall, or even the horizon. On the third night, their endeavors were rewarded. The crew spotted lights converging and then separating—fishing boats intersecting and then moving apart near the shore. At first they wondered if they were hallucinating, as this had become the norm. But the fact that they all saw them buoyed their spirits and renewed their resolve. That was when the last storm hit.

> It was horrendous. Same kind of conditions. Freezing rain, wind, huge waves. But this time, we kind of felt like superheroes. We'd survived a lot and at that point it actually felt like it was us against the elements and we were triumphantly plowing through regardless of the severity of the storm. I remember saying to myself on watch, "OK. We're gonna do this." It felt like an adventure, and although I was terrified, I was also determined. I felt invincible.

Cape Hatteras forms one of the most treacherous shorelines on the mid-Atlantic coast. The crew dropped anchor just off the lighthouse. Unbeknownst to them, it was the most dangerous place of all, for it left the boat exposed to savage and unpredictable crosscurrents. Locals began to gather on the beach and coast guard crews arrived on the scene just in time to see the men jump from the dinghy without their life jackets.

> We weren't thinking too clearly by that point. Someone yelled, "Jump! The next wave will tip us!" And I was the only one with a life jacket. Forty-degree water and riptides that pulled us under time and again. They clung to the oars, and finally, after what seemed like an eternity, we got within five feet from shore and collapsed. The fishermen and coast guard dragged us out. We were exhausted. For me, it was a transcendent moment, mixed with this enormous fatigue. I remember kissing the sand, feeling the wet sand on my lips and just whispering to myself, "Ground." It felt like the most fundamental thing, to be back on land. The next I

recall, I was being lifted into this fisherman's truck for the ride to the naval hospital. Someone had thrown a uniform and hat on me, about three sizes too big. I was hypothermic. My temperature was ninety-three degrees. I was practically delusional. When I got to the hospital, they threw me in the hot shower for over an hour.

The ordeal was over. After eight days at sea, the four were weak, but safe. They rented rooms in a small motel and ventured into the small town only for meals at a neighborhood diner. Each in private contemplation, they talked little, but shared the solidarity of survivors. Rebecca called home, only to find that her mother's experience in the last week added to her sense of the bizarre.

> She told me that the night we turned over in the boat, the first night out, she panicked and began running through the house. When my father was finally able to calm her enough, she told him I was in terrible danger. Then she said, "But Rebecca will be all right, and she'll call next Friday." That was the day I called. When she heard my voice, she said, "I was expecting a call from you today." I remember the hair standing up on my head as I listened to her.

The crew stayed in Cape Hatteras for a week. While lying in bed or sipping hot tea at the diner, Rebecca would review the adventure in her mind. She'd feel herself back in the boat for a few moments, and the power of memory would trigger an involuntary shudder. Then she would recover, notice her surroundings, and return to the simple appreciation for being alive and the gratitude she felt for the locals who had become so protective.

> They were really kind, and excited too. Nothing ever happened in the winter there! They spent a lot of time with us and made us feel welcome. They would laugh, watching us

try to walk again. Everyone could see us coming. I guess we were pretty hilarious without our land legs. We were walking virtually sideways for the first few days. It was a very elastic period and mostly I remember feeling a lot of equanimity and great appreciation for what the people of the town were doing. It was almost a blissful state. I had no concerns whatsoever.

Over time, Rebecca noticed a pattern to her musings. Her thoughts seemed to return to her solitary vigils on deck as if they were attempting to preserve each significant moment, each realization forged under tremendous pressure. She marveled at the pivotal insights that seemed responsible not only for her survival, but also for providing fundamental and invaluable insights about the nature of the mind.

It was such a strong experience of the usefulness of mindfulness and awareness. It was one thing to practice it in a meditation retreat, but quite another to learn how completely life-saving it was. I had real tools, and instead of disconnecting and panicking and wondering—"Why me?" —I could cut through that stuff, let it go, and then really be there in the present moment.

It could be arrogance, but I still feel there was such a strong contrast between the sum total of my experience and the sum total of the rest of the crew. I don't think I was that much healthier or stronger than anyone else. The only way I can explain it to myself was the practice.

Perhaps, if we can remember clearly, there are moments in each of our lives when events conspire to reveal certain fundamental truths and a direction becomes clear. For Rebecca, it was through the pedagogy of crisis that she learned the nature of the Call. Its message was lucid and undeniable. One afternoon, sitting again at the Formica lunch table in the diner, she gleaned her life's itinerary.

> I remember a rambling conversation, and then someone in the crew asking me, "What is this stuff you've been doing?" I realized that it was absolutely clear to me that spiritual practice, meditation, was the most important thing I could do in my life. It was *the* thing I wanted to do *with* my life. I had never had an experience that had taught me so much, and I chose, then and there as a goal, to learn to develop that state of mind as much as I could. That's the path I would follow. Everything else I did would have to form around that.

The week passed, and then, without much fanfare, all took their leave—the men back to their families and Rebecca to visit friends in Michigan. The rest of the crew still seemed in shock, alternately fretful and angry. One vowed never to sail again. Rebecca felt differently. If her decision to deepen the practice of meditation wasn't firm enough, the marked difference between her and the rest of the crew upon leaving provided the coup de grâce.

> It was the type of thing that one could walk away from extremely traumatized. There was anger in the group, and a lot of harsh words said, and there was a lot of ground for getting into some heavy neurotic stuff. But I felt that I walked away from the experience clean. There wasn't a big hangover or interpersonal residue. It felt finished, and there wasn't any reason for me to hold on to those people or the situation. I actually didn't feel much emotion about it, and that surprised me. I felt a healthy sense of detachment, like it had been a movie that was very vivid. I thought I should feel more terrified.
>
> I mean, I wasn't eager to get back on a boat that afternoon, but I'd do it now, and by all means, I'd love to sail again. I'm just going to be a lot more careful about who I choose for the next adventure.

ONE

THE SLUMBER

"Midway upon the journey of our life
I found myself within a forest dark,
For the straightforward path had been lost . . ."
—DANTE, *The Divine Comedy*

THE STATUS QUO provides the stage for the entrance of the unexpected and unusual into people's lives. Whether plain or painful, enervated or inspired, our everyday reality forms the backdrop against which we register the odd and the enigmatic. In myths and fairy tales, the status quo is often represented by times of ease and plenty. The Bible tells us Job[1] was a wealthy man:

> Blameless and upright . . . there were borne to him seven sons and three daughters. He had seven thousand sheep, three hundred she asses and very many servants. So that this man was the greatest of all the people in the east.[2]

Similarly, "The Frog King," a classic Grimms' tale, begins:

> Long, long ago, when wishing still could lead to something, there lived a king whose daughters all were beautiful, but the youngest was so beautiful that the sun itself, who had seen so many things, simply marveled every time it shone on her face. Now close to the castle of this king, was a great dark forest. . . .[3]

However idyllic each story's beginning, one can hear the strains of portent. Job's life has nowhere to go but to unravel, and the king lived at the edge of a dark wood to which his youngest daughter is innocently but inexorably drawn. In these tales, the protagonists are as yet untested. Although life on the surface seems consummate, enduring myths and tales caution us not to be so easily seduced.

The trance of everyday life serves as the humble beginning to our journey into the unexpected. The very antithesis of the unusual, we can see its routine sameness as a state of slumber. Absorbed into that somnambulance, we are unaware how (or even that) we could write a different, possibly more satisfying and inspiring, storyline for lives. In Hinduism, the Sanskrit term *maya* is used to denote the veils of illusion that cloud our perception. Hindu psychology asserts that we are veiled in two ways: We cannot see the insubstantiality of the material world, and we are unable to recognize the divine in ourselves. This cardinal illusion clouds everyone's sight to some degree, and as a result, we grasp for the spoils of material success—money, power, possessions, status—often with Sisyphean undertones, instead of realizing that the true, essential, and enduring wealth lay beneath all forms, right here within us. As Wordsworth lamented:

> The world is too much with us; late and soon,
> Getting and spending, we lay waste our powers;
> Little we see in Nature that is ours;
> We have given our hearts away. . . .[4]

The Slumber represents the first stage in our quest for awakening, one that psychiatrist Roger Walsh calls the Stage of

Conventionality. Ubiquitous, it is rarely perceived, for we are so easily swallowed by it.

> In the West it has been described as a shared hypnosis, consensus trance, or collective psychosis. This impairment or clouding of the mind tends to go unnoticed because we all share in it.[5]

The Slumber can vary infinitely in its form. Some of those I interviewed were clearly suffering before the entrance of the unexpected: a life compromised by addiction; a near-fatal accident or illness; a pervasive and unbridgeable experience of isolation. There were others whose lives proceeded rather evenly. Only during periods of rest could they feel a faint dissatisfaction gnawing at the edges of their awareness. Routine had replaced spontaneity, and habit began to drown a sense of adventure. Sometimes, people were not clear whether they were determining the direction of their lives, or, in fact, being led by a momentum created long before.

When I began this research, I called for people from all walks of life who had experiences that lay dramatically outside their sense of the possible. I imagined that there would be a strong concordance in the tales people reported, but I was surprised to discover that nearly all of those interviewed shared a common characteristic in relation to their lives *before* the event occurred. Looking back, they all saw themselves suspended in place or stuck, in need of a fundamental shift in both the direction and the quality of their lives. This proved to be a near-universal characteristic of the Slumber. Each person, in his or her own way, described common features of this holding period as including:

- a sense that something important was missing;
- a feeling of one's life out of balance, and a consequent overemphasis on one part of their lives;
- a feeling of spinning wheels—a lot of activity perhaps, but a sense of decreasing depth and satisfaction; and
- a feeling that what was once meaningful and attractive had begun to feel empty.

For everyone, to paraphrase Saint-Exupéry, "What was essential was invisible to the eye."[6]

Christopher

A TALE OF SURRENDER

To everyone who knew him, Christopher seemed the epitome of confidence. Young and forthright, with a gift for inspiring people and bringing them together with humor, he had become a leader in the fields of community relations and mental health service delivery. Christopher was a dashing presence, tall and lean, with powder-blue eyes, long reddish-blond hair, and an affection for jeans and cowboy boots, even at work. Well liked, Christopher found his time very much in demand. One day would find him defusing gang rivalry in the schools, while the next he would spend in the offices of city hall, consulting to the mayor or the chief of police.

Christopher's story continues our journey into the unexpected and into the quest it inspires. His tale provides a portrait of accomplishment and a sense of limitless professional potential. Yet, as he entered his thirties, a disquiet began to grow. He began to suspect that despite his success, each achievement would lead only to the next, all within the same sphere of his life. Although he could work harder or become more influential, he grew dubious that it would lead him deeper into the mystery that was himself. Something important was missing.

> I was running a family therapy program for juvenile delinquents and a treatment program for teenage alcoholics. I was a consultant in Washington, D.C., with the National Institute of Alcohol Abuse. I was a consultant to a number of indigenous tribes in Alaska, *and* I was the chairperson of the Delinquency Prevention Commission and rewriting the juvenile justice codes for the entire county! But I was relatively young to be doing all of these things. While the work was valuable to the community, after many years of this level of frenzied activity, I started to feel overwhelmed. It was exhilarating and affirming but it was exhausting. And it was all very much outward directed. I started to feel lost.

Christopher's story is striking because, unlike many others I've heard, the prelude to a major life change was not great suffering and unhappiness, but rather the fulfillment of a cultural ideal. Christopher was young, attractive, and wielded considerable power, influence, and esteem. To the outsider, it seemed an admirable life, one worthy of respect, and even perhaps envy. Still, the status quo period, regardless of whether it is comprised of spectacular success or abject failure, is an imperfect mirror: It reflects the surface, but misses the more fundamental truths that lay below.

Christopher was surrounded by equally driven people, and he found it difficult to describe the ephemeral sensation that something felt off. He hadn't yet learned how to communicate his incipient confusion, especially amid such success. Instead, he sought refuge in greater activity, and drugs.

> I tried many different things to try to find my place, whether it was sexual relationships, or adding one more job description to my plate, or doing various kinds of drug or alcohol combinations, in order to find some bearing, some rudder in the midst of all this tumultuous activity. I was doing coke. A little less than $100 a week; two or three drinks in the evening. I was drinking, Jack Daniel's—straight up. I was spending a lot of time out at night.

> It was like those guys on the Ed Sullivan show who kept all those plates going; and I didn't necessarily doubt that I *could* keep the plates going, but there was beginning to be some doubt in my mind as to *whose* plates these were, and what they were doing in the air. And whether it was going to be my job for the rest of my life to just keep these plates going—or whether there was some deeper meaning or purpose to the whole thing.

Questions of meaning and purpose exert a powerful direction to our lives.[7] They urge us to contemplate a future beyond the status quo and propel us beyond the pull back toward the trance of everyday existence. For nearly a half century, therapists and theologians have maintained that meaning and purpose constitute one of the cornerstones of psychological health. Existential psychotherapists assert that even in less dire circumstances, during the inevitable transitional periods of our lives, the search for meaning and its consequent sense of purpose creates a psychological resilience that enables us to confront, rather than retreat from, the unknown.

Christopher began to ask himself questions about meaning and purpose. He allowed himself to feel the fatigue in his body, and behind that, the poverty in his spiritual life. He began to wonder about his future and the possibility that, regardless of how successful he was, there was something deeper toward which to strive, or more accurately, into which to surrender.

> I remember saying to my secretary one day, "You know, I realized that, between houseguests or roommates or meetings and conferences, I hadn't spent a night by myself, alone, in about three years!" So I got this inspiration to go away by myself for three days just so I could listen to whatever was going on in there—to who I was as a *being* rather than who I was as a performer, or an actor, or as someone who has accomplished a lot. I remember feeling as if this was really an enormous step for me . . . to spend three whole days by myself!

Christopher canceled his appointments and prepared for his small sojourn. Although the change of seasons is subtle in Southern California, it somehow felt like the right time of year for introspection.

> I guess everybody has times of the year when, for them, they are particularly open to reflecting on how their life is going and what might be coming next. I wasn't conscious of it then, but as I reflected on times before that and since, it seems that's the case for me, in early December. Sort of a time when the veil lifts a little bit.

For the first time in years, Christopher felt called to someplace quiet and absent of stimulation. He left his briefcase at home and provided no forwarding number to his staff. He wasn't sure exactly what he wanted from his quest, but he was certain that he needed to be alone.

> The Oaks Motel. It was not a high-class establishment. No pool, no phone, one small bed. It was just a motel on the side of a road. I certainly wasn't gonna be entertained while I was there. I just went fully intending to do nothing. I stopped at a store on the way and bought what I thought I'd need for the next three days: a drawing pad and a box of

crayons, a bottle of Jack Daniel's, and a used copy of Kazantzakis's *The Last Temptation of Christ.*

> *"Properly understood and applied,*
> *prayer is the most potent instrument of action."*[8]
> —MAHATMA GANDHI

In a small way, Christopher had begun the process of changing his life. Whereas past travels often involved stays at posh hotels, with swimming pools, water bars, and nightlife, this weekend's retreat could not have been more spare.

> And so for three days I basically sat around and read and took walks. I would come back from a walk and I would draw what I saw, or draw what I was feeling, or draw whatever came into my mind. I don't know why I did this. I wasn't an art therapist. I didn't even know what art therapy was. But for some reason or another, this is what I thought I needed to do. So I would draw these pictures of things I saw, or just shapes or colors, or whatever happened to be going on. And then I'd tape them up on the walls around me, and then I'd sit back and I'd pour myself a drink and I'd take a look at these things. Then I'd go back to my book. And then I'd take a nap. And then I'd take a walk again. And you know, it just pretty much went on like that for about three days.

> And I just got quiet. Somehow, through all that, layers of activity began to just melt away. And I actually started to pray. And my prayer essentially was for some kind of guidance, some kind of teaching, which I guess ultimately is really what everybody prays for when they really pray. I wasn't after a Mercedes-Benz. I didn't want a color TV. I just wanted some sense about who I was, and where I was going.

Christopher was new to spiritual practice, and he hadn't yet grasped what was to be set in motion by his simple prayers.

He just knew he needed help. He knew the frenzy of activity that waited for him back in town, and he surmised that, without too much effort, he could be pulled back in and not stop to reflect for perhaps another year. The Call that would summon Christopher was a subtle one, but it was undeniably powerful. On the last night of his retreat, the first of two events occurred that nudged him onto a spiritual path.

> I remember after a relatively fervent period of this kind of prayerful meditation—it was my last night there, Sunday night, I guess—I took a walk around the neighborhood of this motel. There was this church lit up with this cross against the sky, right behind the moon. I was awestruck. It was beautiful. I don't remember falling to my knees or anything, but it just became clear to me that it sort of reflected something that I'd already known—that I had a deep spiritual nature, and that a lot of the drinking and drugs had been covering it up, because I was afraid of what it would mean if I were to become a spiritual person.

Gazing at the cross against the dark blue of the twilight sky, Christopher entered a deep and quiet reverie. Healing in itself, it also contained insights he had long suppressed. Struggling to emerge was a picture of himself, allowing his life to be guided by faith, contemplation, and spiritual practice. The gentle scene of the church suddenly exposed a relationship, where beforehand, Christopher believed he was alone. It was a monumental discovery, and at that moment, the meaning of the experience became clear.

> I remember being struck by the image of the church that evening, and realizing that there was a sort of a dialogue going on here! I had asked a question and here was an answer. Or at least, I had proposed a situation and there was a response. *Clearly,* there was dialogue going on! It was

breathtaking to realize that there are some forces that are bigger than me at work, and that I'm actually a part of those forces.

Christopher felt he had been given a glimpse of a possibility far greater than he had imagined. Perhaps there *were* forces at work whose origins lay outside himself. The idea that some divine intelligence might be sensing his deepest longing seemed almost unbearable in its delight.

You know, in everything that I'd ever been involved in up to that point, I was always the boss, even at a relatively young age. I was the chairman of the commission, or the director of the family therapy program, or the founder of the alcohol treatment center, and so part of the sense of being overwhelmed was the sense that there's *nothing* bigger than me. And it was deeply comforting to feel as if there were something benign and loving that was larger than me that seemed to be listening to my best interests. You know, having grown up in an alcoholic family, that wasn't an experience I had very often in my life. To feel as if there was something bigger than me took a lot of pressure off.

Something had begun to shift. Christopher didn't speak much about his time away, but friends were happy he looked so refreshed. Mostly, when he went home after work, he would sit by himself and continue to listen. A week later, one definitive and unexplainable event provided the catalyst and the guidance he needed. It took less than a few moments, but again, the meaning was unmistakable.

I was sitting on the porch of my house one evening, and right out of the blue came this voice, which I had never heard before and I haven't heard since. I don't remember what I was thinking about, but the voice was quite forceful, and it said, "Don't you *ever* worry about tomorrow!" And I whirled around and yelled, "Who the hell is that?" But there was nobody there. I distinctly heard a voice. It was sort of a stern, parental, exasperated—you know, the way a parent would scold a child, *"Don't you ever! . . ."* But this time it was for my own good. "Don't you *ever* worry about tomorrow." So, I looked around and I just had to laugh, because, I mean, what do you say? "Oh yes, I *will* worry about tomorrow!"

Both the experience of the church and hearing the voice challenged Christopher to review his notion of who was really in charge and what was guiding his life. This was the crack in the door, and the light that entered revealed the possibility of a conversation, one in which his most cherished dreams could be recognized by an intelligence greater and wiser than he.

I prayed for guidance, and then this image shows up of this church silhouetted against the sky. And, you know, regardless of whether it was Christian or non-Christian, it didn't really matter. Clearly, there was something about the whole nature of taking a spiritual path that was being reaffirmed to me.

To those who wrestle with its meaning, the unexpected appears as a harbinger of things to come. The route may be poorly defined, and its consummation cannot be accurately predicted, but if one truly endeavors to follow its meaning, success is eventually assured. At this point in the journey, one significant step emerges for all who have related their tales. For everyone, the unexpected required an act of surrender—of a certain lifestyle, a particular self-image, and often of one's most cherished beliefs about the nature of the world and what is in fact possible in it. Psychologically, emotionally, and cognitively, we must empty ourselves in order to allow for something new.

The unexpected—the beauty of the church at night and the unexplainable voice a week later—yielded a sacred meaning.

Nothing apparent was occurring on the surface, but an important transformation had begun. To his delight, Christopher discovered himself a component part of an adventure, not its leader, and when he responded with excitement and curiosity, a journey was christened.

Christopher felt ready. Although he couldn't glean his final destination, the next step seemed clear and imperative. It took a few months to extricate himself from his vocational responsibilities, and then he began to tour the country, to search for a seminary.

> There were many choices, but I found that the ones on the East Coast appealed to me the most. Harvard contained the Center for World Religions, and courses in liberation theology, which I had begun to read about. I grew up in New York, so I was also seduced by the allure of Harvard's intellectual reputation. The possibility of taking courses throughout the university was a final plus, so it became my first choice. I was thrilled to get in.

Christopher sailed through the required classes in scripture, exegesis, and hermeneutics, as well as the more practical preparations for the ministry and the guidance of a church. But although the theoretical pursuits were interesting, he was most moved by the practice of Christianity at the edges, away from conventional applications of church doctrine.

> I sought out Henri Nouwen, a Christian and a rebel on the faculty, because he had spent a lot of his time in Central and South America, applying the principles of liberation theology and himself being mentored by the father of the movement, Gustav Guttierrez. Henri's idea of the spiritual life was what he called "downward mobility." He felt that priests or ministers, like most everyone, are seduced by power and importance or titles and places of honor, but he taught that a

true spiritual life was one where you offered the best you could, and progressively became less important, even less visible in your works. Now this was really different, especially for such an overachiever like myself. And it was also frightening for the same reasons. Henri was keenly intelligent, with a big heart. He was my first true spiritual mentor.

The three years of formal education had passed quickly, and although there was no doubt that he made the right choice in entering the seminary, Christopher was at a loss to understand exactly what being called, in this context, meant. And while his classmates entertained interviews by representatives of various denominations and began to share the excitement of graduation, Christopher hesitated.

> I was much more interested in being a priest in the world than to a small select group of people whose main concern was necessarily maintaining membership. I was dubious that Jesus would consider it very useful in the larger world. I wrestled with this a lot in seminary. I believed that being "called" to the ministry meant that I would have to change myself—act more holy, straightlaced, predictable, reliable—all those things you expect ministers to be. It didn't seem a whole lot different than any upper-level job in a big corporation!

Unbeknownst to him, Christopher had been here before. He had decided to enter the ministry in order to extricate himself from his life in California and the roles that began to constrict him, but now, peering down the road, he was wary of the same eventuality, just cloaked in different robes.

> So what did ordination mean? What did it mean for me to have been called by the image of the church, and the voice on my porch? It was only toward the end of seminary that I realized something very important. I realized that if God called me, then it was *me* that was being called—me with

my bizarre sense of humor, my weird New York take on things; my charisma and my slothfulness; my tendency to jump into things unprepared. I realized that being called meant that God would be able to use all of this quirkiness. When I finally became ordained, I wore red, high-top sneakers to make a point that I was being ordained *as* a priest, not ordained into *becoming* a priest, and that was an important distinction for me.

The insight seemed to set him free, and upon graduation, Christopher left the country for a stay in Peru, working with radical Catholics and ministering to the poor. Whether sleeping on the floors in the mountain huts of the Andes or visiting the pueblo hovens, the border towns just outside Lima, Christopher reveled in a spirituality that was tested in the trenches. Prayer meetings, poetry, and politics took their place side by side as the definition of the ministry seemed to shift to whatever was most needed—procuring food for the hungry, reciting scriptures for the sick, or helping to repair water mains and electrical lines after the periodic mayhem caused by local terrorists. This was real work, and Christopher felt inspired and cleansed.

Christopher's story exemplifies the progression of stages in the Stages of Transformation: the trance of the status quo, dissolving that trance through the entry of the unexpected, a subsequent period of separation from the everyday world in which one contemplates the meaning of the unexpected and the journey it has launched. The passage completes its cycle with one's return to the world. It is here that one applies what was learned during the adventure, and for those who have made the journey, their choices bear a stamp of individuality and iconoclasm. No two life passages are exactly alike, and people find their confidence and sense of direction not through the dictates of the cultural norm, but from the experience of having plumbed their depths and emerged with a unique perspective of themselves and of their relationship to the larger world.

But Christopher's tale is also instructive in that it shows us that life's deepest lessons need to be learned, not once, but many times. Psychological growth may not be so much the accumulation of new information or confronting new challenges, but revisiting central life themes again and again in different guises, at different stages of the life cycle. Rather than digging twenty wells, one foot in depth, in our search for water, revisiting major life themes offers the opportunity to dig one hole, twenty feet deep, and thereby ensures success—maximum understanding at the greatest depth.

Upon his return, Christopher sidestepped the trappings of traditional clerical life. Instead, he endeavored to transpose his expertise in a variety of ways, to a number of rural communities in northern New Mexico. On Sunday morning, he was just as likely to be ministering to the dying in Española, or helping to build a playground for local children in Chamisal or Chimayo, as guest preaching in front of a congregation.

> Ever since I left Peru, I've been reconfiguring some mix of psychology, spirituality, and community organizing. I was seeing clients in a small private practice, but I didn't want to feel isolated in the consulting room. I felt we needed to include everyone in the community, so I took a certain amount of the money made in my psychotherapy practice and devoted it to community projects. Eventually that became a foundation. We now raise over $200,000 a year that we just give away. I also began working with AIDS patients. There were so many memorial services for people who were dying, and the bizarre thing to me was, that at this time, in the mid-1980s many gays and many people with AIDS were not even allowed in some churches. So I began to create a service of Thanksgiving for those with AIDS. We would com-

mandeer an auditorium, and the service was specifically intended to celebrate that even in the crucible of that suffering,
there was some grace, some opening, honesty, or kindness
that was born.

Christopher's work was laudable by any standards. He was
recognized as a valuable community resource, and he spent the
better part of the next decade applying his particular brand of
theology—offering workshops and classes, holding services and
ceremonies, and shepherding his charitable activities toward the
greatest need. But Christopher was no longer a young adult,
and with two children of his own and an active family life, it
seemed that an increasing amount of his efforts were swallowed
by elaborate attempts at time management and the balancing of
too many commitments. Incrementally, and beneath his awareness, Christopher had once again been seduced by his talents.

> I created a whirlwind of activity and accomplishment that
> was growing beyond my capacity. All the things I was in-
> volved in were good, but it was just too much and I had,
> again, misjudged the level of my involvement. It was virtually
> a mirror image to my life in Santa Barbara, just before I
> landed in the Oaks Motel. And then I got sick.

The streptococcal strain has proven to be pneumonia's most
virulent form. Left undiagnosed and untreated for even a few
days, the virus invades the circulatory system, rendering the
blood septic. Shortly thereafter, pleurisy develops. The fluid that
rapidly fills the lungs makes speech agonizing and breathing
nearly impossible. Christopher had been attending a worship
service near Taos. He had a cold but, hearty throughout his life,
he paid it little heed. Just after returning home, his condition
worsened.

It was early September, still pretty hot in New Mexico, and I was shivering. Nothing seemed to help. My temperature climbed to 105 degrees. I called a friend who was a doctor, and quickly, he admitted me to the hospital—in serious condition. They told me it was the same form of pneumonia that Jim Henson died of so suddenly, and for a number of days, it wasn't clear if I would survive.

Mostly, he slept, only to be awoken by nurses and respiratory therapists. Conversation left him literally breathless, and it seemed that there was actually very little to say. Although his body struggled to combat the disease, Christopher found himself tranquil.

> I noticed I wasn't afraid of dying at all. I certainly had been at other times, but now, I didn't really care. I was either gonna die or I wasn't, but there was nothing I could do about it. It wasn't indifference or apathy. It was different than that. I was totally powerless in that bed, like it or not, and it seemed the only real choice was to surrender into how things seemed to be going rather than fighting it.

> It turned out that during the previous summer, a number of people had been admitted with streptococcal pneumonia, and they had died because it was so rare and it took too long to make the diagnosis. By the time I arrived, the staff recognized what I had, and they had the routine down. So, you know, some of the people who died before me contributed to the knowledge that saved me; so intricate is the web of life.

The unexpected had once again visited Christopher, this time in a deadly form. And although with both the illness and the enormous array of medication made it difficult to think even a few cogent thoughts, Christopher sensed that there was meaning to be gleaned, should he survive. For weeks, he could not speak without requiring minutes to recover his breath. It took longer for him to walk again without great fatigue, and in total, six months were necessary for his complete convalescence. It was impossible for Christopher to resume his normal activity, and it created a time apart—a distanced platform from which to review his life.

> It became very clear to me that the meaning of this was that my life was out of balance. The residual teaching and benefit was the experience of surrender. Surrender is the thing I got in the cells of my body because, for awhile, my survival was just not up to me. It meant letting go, or rather letting "be" how things seem to be evolving and not fighting circumstance so much. Now, I don't know if God threw down a bolt of streptococcal pneumonia into my body, I don't know if there is that kind of causality, but my experience of surrender was so strong and it was so potent that it's guided me ever since. I have yet to lose that awareness, and it has now become the criteria with which I decide what I take on. The path for me is now almost universally determined by the degree of surrender I can bring to it.

During our first interview, Christopher still lived in the hills outside of Santa Fe. The site of our last conversation, however, took place on the porch of an old rented cabin, just a few yards from the beach, in northern California. It was late February. The afternoon sun felt warm and there was a distinct hint of spring in the air. Rhododendrons and azalea had begun to bud, and already, the petals of sea lavender and catmint had opened into lazy spirals of small blue and indigo petals. An old collie dozing in the sun across the sandy road lifted its head to watch a blue jay, and then sank back into sleep.

Christopher looked over the water, and then to the sharply raked mountains to the east. He drew a deep breath of the moist coastal breeze, a delight he would no longer take for granted.

And so I guess that brings us up to date. I'm on sabbatical now, and I'll be here for six months or so. During the first months of my recovery, my bad health was an ally in helping me say "no" to things. By the end of that time, I learned to give myself permission to be more judicious in choosing what I did. I've declined almost all commitments at this point. It's a natural continuation of the teaching I was getting from my illness. I'm learning to slow down and disengage, and to listen very carefully to where I might be needed, rather than just stay on the same track and pare down a bit, which is what most of us do when we want to change our lives. Too many of us involved in doing good in the world, do good very badly. I think it's because we don't live with enough quiet, and we go around trying to fix things without really knowing what will actually be healing. So I'm learning to be quiet, and I believe the next right thing will emerge from that.

My days are pretty simple. I write a bit in the morning and night, and a few times a day, take a walk on the beach. I've begun to pray while I'm walking—the rhythm and the wind seem a perfect accompaniment. Sometimes I'll recite the Lord's Prayer, or a psalm, or a simple meditation of healing or loving kindness for people I know who are in need. It's funny, but after all those years of highly visible activity, this now forms a big part of my day. I consider it my work.

Our conversation drew to a natural close. After the intense concentration of the interview, our eyes left one another and lifted to a red-tailed hawk, hovering a thousand feet above us near a cliff. It had found the precise place where it could float on the sea breeze and look to the horizon, its wings quiet and still.

TWO

THE CALL

"If a man could pass through Paradise in a dream, and have a flower presented to him as a pledge that his soul had really been there, and if he found that flower in his hand when he awoke—Ay! and what then?"
—SAMUEL TAYLOR COLERIDGE

"The real is only one realization of the possible."
—ILYA PRIGOGINE, winner of the Nobel Prize in chemistry

LIGHTNING PLUMMETS from the sky at about seventy-five miles per second. The air in a cumulonimbus formation becomes polarized, each side poised like titanic armies ready to clash, negative ions gather lower to the ground, positive ions on high. As the bolt nears the ground, electrical discharges called streamers arise from trees, mountaintops, or power lines—as if summoned. At the precise point where these streamers intersect the bolt, a brilliant white flash arrests the night and silhouettes the terrain. A rebounding stroke now ascends skyward, but this time, it is exponentially more powerful, approaching speeds of 50,000 miles per second, charges up to 100,000 watts, and temperatures of 30,000° Kelvin. This bolt literally rips the air, leaving behind a vacuum, and then thunder, the moan of the heavens, in its wake.

During these moments, we stop. Normal routines are abandoned to the superordinate luminescence of the flash, and the primal concussion of thunder. It is simply impossible to go on as before. Nothing is as it was. Normal no longer exists. The sky, a forbidding gray, presses upon us, the ozone-filled atmosphere becomes an eerie rose, and the explosion of blue-white light renders stark and skeletal the comfortable contours of the familiar landscape.

The thunderbolt has been recognized throughout the ages as the spark of the divine, a moment of illumination from a heavenly source. In the Hindu pantheon, lightning is related to the glance of Shiva, the destroyer of all material forms. In Judeo-Christian iconography, the Divine is hidden from our sight, and the lightning's flash momentarily reveals God in his active and sometimes terrible might. Some myths reveal not only the power of heavenly forces in relation to man, but the actual process by which the thunderbolt arrives into our lives. In Chinese myth, the Mother of Lightning, Tien Mu appears magnificently robed in blue, green, red, and white. She holds two mirrors, one in each hand. Where the reflections of the two mirrors cross, lightning will crackle and flash.[1] What are these two mirrors? What do they reflect? This myth speaks to us about the process of spiritual illumination and of a dialogue between heaven and earth. One of Tien Mu's mirrors reflects the mortal world and the other, the celestial. And just as the streamer arises from a tree or mountain seeking the downward burst of the bolt to create illumination in the sky, so does the intersection of the secular and sacred—our earth-boundedness and a divinity or greater intelligence—create illumination in our own lives.

In Greek mythology, Jupiter holds three thunderbolts. They

symbolize Chance, Destiny, and Providence—the forces that when brought together craft our future.[2]

The Call is certainly the most dramatic stage to explore in the Stages of Transformation. It heralds a major awakening. It demands our attention; arouses a yearning for something deeper and more essential in our lives; beckons us to a higher level of courage and creativity; and by invoking a quest, summons us to pursue our life's purpose or dream. Should we rise to the challenge, we gain entry to a depth of symbolism, vitality of spirit, and range of possibility that lie far beyond what we have known.

Each of those who so candidly shared their stories with me had an experience of the thunderbolt. Some adventures like Rebecca's voyage and Christopher's illness were so powerful that they crashed through the roofs and shook the foundations of their normal lives, rendering simple explanations difficult and a retreat into "life as it was before" impossible. For others, as we shall hear, the flash was more subtle but no less powerful, appearing with an uncanny intimacy, speaking directly to a central question that had gone unanswered, for days, months, even a lifetime.

Remember, those whom I sought had not only experienced something radically unusual that fell far beyond what they thought possible, but based on those experiences, they had fundamentally changed their lives. (There were actually many I spoke to who had unusual experiences, but far less for whom those experiences became the catalyst for deep change.) What did this subset of people have in common? Was it enough for them to have experienced the unexpected, or were there other features they shared, less obvious perhaps, but significant? Those who made fundamental changes in their lives following their experience with the unexpected recognized—either during those moments or shortly thereafter—that what was happening to them contained meaning, though they might not have been able to articulate it well at the time. For some, the serendipity of surprises was heavenly, filled with grace and light. For others, the unexpected trespassed into their world and was accompanied by sadness, confusion, and even terror. Regardless of the valence of the event, however, each knew, on a level deep and inexpressible, that their experience was "a Call."

Tara

GRANDFATHER IS CALLING

"Sometimes in the evening I sit, looking out on the big Missouri. The sun sets, and dusk steals over the water. In the shadows I seem to see our Indian village, with smoke curling upward from the earth lodges, and in the river's roar I hear the yells of the warriors, and the laughter of little children as of old. I am an old woman now. The buffalo and blacktail deer are gone, and our Indian ways are almost gone. Sometimes I find it hard to believe that I ever lived them."

—WAHEENEE, HIDATSA *(North Dakota)*[3]

I am a Cree-Blackfoot. When I was four, my parents divorced and my father took me all over the West. I led a kick-around life. I never lived in a place more than two years till I was thirty-five. Mostly, I was with my father who was a cowboy and a jack-of-all-trades, or in a Catholic boarding school.

Tara's story speaks of a profound disconnection—from her family, her tribe, and ultimately, herself. But hers is a also a story of reconnection and of two clarion calls that led to finding her emotional, filial, and spiritual center—or more accurately, it finding her.

Tara was virtually orphaned when young. Native American by birth, she had little exposure to her rich heritage. Although she had blood ties to a spiritual tradition that thrived on the education of its children through ritual and allegory—and that passed down these teachings through the lineage by elders— her family circumstances denied her that bounty. Born in Montana, she wouldn't enjoy a permanent home until she had children of her own.

Tara is now in her mid-fifties. A woman of uncommon beauty, with rich black hair and deep-set blue eyes, she has a somewhat formal but self-effacing manner. She speaks with an understatement that is archetypal to her clan. One can sense in her a palpable, but unself-conscious, dignity.

> I spent some time with my Indian grandmother, but she was an orphan and felt she couldn't offer me the traditions. She felt a great loss for what she didn't have, but she did plant seeds. Those seeds slept underground in me for many years.

Tara's early life is a portrait of rootlessness. The absence of both a stable family and an extended tribal network left her feeling unwanted and alienated—and different from the children she met, whether they were native or not. Her tenures in boarding schools were especially vexing due to a double stigma, as an Indian and as a child of a broken home. Here, the feelings of abandonment cut most deep. Somewhere buried, Tara carried an unnameable but tangible feeling of something lost.

Most of the children felt they had been set aside in some way, and we all seemed so isolated from one another. Some schools were better than others, but all of them were hard on the children. I had a particularly hard time making friends because we had moved so much and I think it drove me deeper inside. I felt deserted.

Tara rarely saw her mother, and although her stays with her father were exciting, they were not very intimate. Her grandmother offered a promise of connection to a larger family, but she too had been cut off and shared Tara's sense of drift. Without an even elementary sense of who she was and to whom she belonged, Tara's adolescence became an emotionally precarious one. Just seventeen, she married a dental student at the local university, and aspired to redress what, for so long, had been missing: a family.

I wanted to become a good Catholic, middle-class housewife and mother. So I had six children in six years! I tried to be very good—good in the sense that I was very self-sacrificing—but I had virtually no sense of knowing who I really was.

Through the years, I became very unhappy. My husband was totally involved in his life as a practicing dentist. Once again I felt isolated and, in addition, overwhelmed with so many children.

Soon after her sixth child, Tara left the marriage. She imagined taking her children and finding someone who would care, not only for them, but for her. An ugly divorce ensued, however, and without the resources necessary to procure expert legal representation, she lost custody of all six children. The agony of losing them seemed limitless enough, but that pain also triggered into the emotional vertigo she felt as a child, and the cumulative effect left her bewildered, distraught, and wanting to run to anyone who could promise moments of relief and an opportunity to forget.

> He was a fashion photographer. He was also an official at the local racetrack. Before we were married, he treated me like a queen. I got all the attention my first husband was unable to give me. I thought it was the answer to all my prayers.

Tara began to believe that the only way she could cope with her loss was to become a different person. Purposely, as if to rectify each ill from her past, she created a list of remedies. Having felt so invisible during both her childhood and her first marriage, she sought work in which she could be noticed and admired. To assuage a deep sense of inadequacy, Tara aspired to become someone attractive and alluring. Finally, to remedy the years laboring dutifully but uninspired as a mother of six, she was drawn to a high-profile life in the fast lane.

> I became a model in Seattle. It was all about power, money, and sex. I needed people to feed back to me that I was attractive and that I was OK and worthwhile. For awhile, it was pretty exciting. My husband and I spent a lot of time at the racetrack, and it was romantic, glamorous, and lots of high living. It was crazy, but I felt I had missed out on some adventure in the first marriage, with all the children, and this really seemed seductive for awhile.

> But after a few years of that, it became a very downward spiral, and I began to fall apart. We were moving seasonally with the racetrack, and were surrounded with people who based their interests and activities around drinking and gambling, and everything that goes with that. My husband became an alcoholic, and I began to drink as well. I missed my children terribly. I had a daughter with my second husband, and I poured all of the affection toward my other children into her. She was the love of my life, but I was

already having a number of serious physical and emotional problems. I began to feel I made a terrible mistake marrying my second husband, and I was experiencing great pain in my abdomen.

It was as if Tara was running from room to room on the same floor of a building, unable either to go higher or to descend beneath the form of her life and discover who, in fact, she really was. Both her body and mind unraveled in her confusion. Upon consultation, Tara's physician had proffered his diagnosis and recommended surgery. Her body was weak, and she suffered from marked hormonal imbalances that left her drained and depressed. Although still quite young, seven births in eight years proved too much. Given the degree of uterine distress, it was suggested that she have a hysterectomy.

It was to be a simple hysterectomy, but the recovery didn't go as planned. I was sent home, but within twenty-four hours after the surgery an ambulance rushed me back to the hospital. I was bleeding to death. They operated five times in the next three days, but they couldn't stop the flow of blood. After the last operation, the surgeon called my husband and said, "John, you have a half hour to get here before she dies. Don't be late!" Shortly after that, I died.

> They are sending a voice to me.
> From the place where the sun goes down,
> Our Grandfather is sending a voice to me.
> From where the sun goes down,
> They are talking to me as they come.
> Our Grandfather's voice is calling to me.
> That winged One there where the Giant lives,
> Is sending a voice to me. He is calling me.
> Our Grandfather is calling me![4]
>   Prayer from Sacred Pipe Ceremony

[What happened] was typical, but I didn't know until years
later. I didn't know anything about these things at the time.

Tara's husband was late in arriving at the hospital. No act
of grace could squeeze him through downtown Seattle traffic
at rush hour. Had he been present, however, he, like the
physicians and nurses attending to Tara, would have seen the
same thing: A young woman, once so vibrant and beautiful
that her face was familiar in fashion magazines, now lay lifeless
on the hospital gurney, her cheeks gaunt and her complexion
blanched of its deep olive tone. There was no movement, no
breath. Even sophisticated monitors failed to record the impulses of life.

But that was on the outside. For a duration of time that no
one, including Tara, could estimate, something quite different
was occurring within.

> I seemed to be falling down a tube toward a beautiful soft,
> white light. I was moving very rapidly, but I wasn't afraid.
> Then I arrived at the light. I felt embraced by it. I felt like
> I was free. It was a kind of freedom greater than anything
> I'd ever experienced—a spiritual freedom. There had been
> so much physical and emotional pain during my life, espe-
> cially after losing my children and the five surgeries. I was
> to the point of just defending myself from the pain from one
> moment to the next. I didn't know how to get out.

> In the light, I felt I actually succeeded at something. I suc-
> ceeded in finally escaping an existence that had always been
> filled with obstacles. In the light, it was different. I was
> finally out of prison.

Tara had never been exposed to writings or testimonials
about near-death experiences, but hers was classic: Having medically died, she seemed to journey through a tunnel, emerging

through a portal into a space filled with a warm and inviting light. The drama of the preceding moments—the flurry of medical interventions and the accompanying emotional intensity—seemed to slip away, and she was simply aware of being held, suspended, and safe.

The obstacles to scientific research at the moment of death are daunting, and to date, physicians and psychologists still know relatively little about precisely what is occurring here. Are these images simply the final firings of synapses? Does the mind, in its last micro-moments, offer images of peace and rest, an evolutionary attempt to dispel the fear of the vast incomprehensible nothingness that is the end of life? Or is it possible that a state between life and death exists, a netherworld where we are prepared for an immense transition, and even met by loved ones and deities who offer compassion and guidance. First-person accounts from throughout the world are remarkably similar in form and detail, but rather than proving one theory over another, this seems to support the possibility of all three: physiological, psychological, and spiritual.

Neither scientific analysis of the data nor hypothesis testing were in Tara's thoughts, however, when she heard a voice so foreign yet so intimate, it pierced her heart.

It was masculine and sounded extremely loving and patient, but the message was very hard for me to accept. The voice said, "You need to go back." I was feeling I was finally out and free, and there was no way . . . and while I didn't have an image of having a body, it seemed like I was stomping my feet and yelling, "You can't make me! I'm out and I won't go back!" That's when the voice truly shocked me.

With great patience, great loving patience, he said: "No one can make you do anything. This is part of what you need to learn." He said, "One of the reasons you have come here is to learn that you have free will." Until then I didn't have a sense of that in my life. I was always at the effect of other people. So he said, "Nobody can make you do anything, but if you don't go back, because you've come into this life to do certain things, you will have to repeat your life, re-experience your childhood, and come back to this point."

It was difficult to argue. The tone was so tender that Tara had trouble dismissing the counsel out of hand. Further, the message within her *hejira*—her mystical journey—seemed para-doxical, in such a profound way, that she realized she was being guided.

> I knew almost nothing about reincarnation. I was raised Cath-olic, so that was certainly not supported there. But I realized very clearly that this was what I was being taught. And given that, it also made a lot of sense. I mean, the thought of going through *my* childhood again was too much! There wasn't any arguing with this voice. I said, "All right, I'll come back," and as soon as I said that, I was back in my body in the hospital.

The unexpected calls us. Whether voices or visions, mo-ments of terror or moments of grace, they are imperatives to awaken and injunctions to embark on a quest to reveal the deeper, truer nature of a world in which such fantastic and unexplainable events are possible. "How could this happen?" "What does this mean?" These were the questions that pro-pelled those I interviewed into the quest.

Tara had come to my attention through her husband, a gifted physical therapist named Dan who was teaching a series of seminars in San Francisco. Her response to my initial query was a gentle one, accepting the invitation to be interviewed with interest and modesty, but with no particular reference to the extraordinary nature of her experiences. Tara, in fact, had three such experiences during this time in her life. The second came just after she realized she had "returned" to the emergency room.

> The facts argue with my memory here, but I remember waking up and answering a phone call for me. I know now that my arms had been strapped to the gurney so that obviously this was an image I had. The funny thing is, however, that the journey I took next seemed connected to finally stopping the internal bleeding, something that five surgeries were unable to accomplish.

Tara heard another voice on the other end of the line. This time it was female, and she sounded much older. Again, the voice was kind, but it was also direct and purposeful and it enjoined Tara to follow her instructions faithfully.

> It sounded like an elder woman's voice. She said if I followed her directions, she would help me. And then she took me down into my uterus. I could see it from the inside and I could see that it was still bleeding. It was like a subterranean cave with cracks in the walls, and water or moisture dripping through. She told me to extend my finger and draw it along these cracks, and that if I did that, the bleeding would stop. Then she said, "Let me know when the dripping is all finished"!

> When I was done, she gave me a Christian prayer thanking Jesus, one I hadn't known. The next thing I knew, I woke up and was told the bleeding had stopped. I was discharged the next day. They said there was no reason to keep me any longer.

Myths and tales throughout the world are replete with protagonists who, about to embark upon a quest for meaning, are helped by a guiding spirit or protective figure. It may be a loving and wise fairy godmother, as for Cinderella, who offers aid when all others have responded with indifference or cruelty. Or a young beauty like Ariadne, who, having fallen in love with Theseus at first sight, devises a way for him to escape the deathly confines of the labyrinth, lair of the man-eating Minotaur. Often, the helper is an elder—a chrone, hermit, or wizard. In the tales of King Arthur, Merlin is the presiding guide and mentor well into Arthur's old age. In Hopi creation myths, Grandmother Spider leads primitive insects, then higher animals, and eventually humans, into successively lighter and less forbidding worlds. Her charge from Tawa, the Sun Spirit, is to help the beings of the earth learn to understand the meaning of life.

If myths provide a template for the structure of a quest, suffering is often the catalyst. It may be a disease of the body that calls to be healed or a constriction of the mind such as a long-standing bitterness or anger that must be dissolved. Quests are inaugurated because an emergent sense of freedom has been too long surpressed (for instance, the Exodus from the land of Egypt). There is a poverty or emptiness in our lives (a blight upon the land; a kingdom whose fields have gone fallow; the royal couple is infertile) that must be examined and (the Gods must be appeased) our relationship to the divine transformed. The quest begins with a Call: "Ripples on the surface of life, produced by unsuspected springs . . . very deep—as deep as the soul itself."[5] This is the Call to Adventure that Joseph Campbell describes at the beginning of the heroic journey; the first steps toward the execution of one's destiny, where "the herald or announcer of the adventure . . . is often dark or loathing, terrifying or judged evil by the world; yet if one could follow, the way would be opened through the walls of day into the dark where the jewels glow."[6]

Tara knew she had passed through the portal of critical illness into the light beyond, but she had no frame of reference for her experience. Out of mortal danger, she returned home having lost much weight and feeling weak. Yet something puzzled her. Her physicians felt so confident that medical treatment worked that it made her suspicious. Nowhere in the scientific model could she find explanations for these two momentous experiences. The spark that had ignited would not be extinguished.

> I was frail at first but began to recover very quickly. I just looked at what happened and had to believe it was true. Something happened there that changed my life. There was just no getting beyond those two memories and that they changed what was happening to me. No one thought I'd live. In fact, they thought I died!

The Call can arise with such power that its repercussions may dramatically upend our lives. Unsatisfying circumstances may no longer seem tolerable, and where once we may have lacked the courage to act on our own behalf, we now find both the fortitude and conviction. Tara could simply not go on as before. Her former life was suddenly revealed in its triviality, and she was now certain there were deeper paths to traverse.

> The moment I left the hospital, I began to leave my husband and the life we had fallen into. The decision was clear. It was just a matter of how. I felt that I made a powerful decision when I said, "All right, I'll come back." I realized that I knew what the light was. It was the realization that I had choice and free will. I began to meet people who could answer some of my questions. I just seemed to gravitate to them. They seemed so much more attractive than anyone else in my life. It was the first time I felt good about myself . . . probably the first time I experienced anything like

self-esteem. And I was sharing stories—listening to others and telling them mine.

Tara had made a powerful choice, but it wasn't obvious from her recounting. Yes, she realized the vacuousness of life at the racetrack and had experienced its destructive effects. Her decision to leave her husband therefore seemed understandable. She also needed to dissolve the isolation in which she had imprisoned herself. But the motivation for her emancipation came from a much deeper source. Tara decided that what happened to her had *meaning,* and with that decision, the trajectory of her future, if not the details of the journey, had become clear. Her survival was a testament to the realization that she could make choices on her own behalf, and that, when she did, some surprising things happened. "And if there was truth in what I was told by that voice about choice and free will," she reasoned, "then the second half of the message—that I have come into this life to do certain things—must also be true."

Tara's relationship to the world had fundamentally changed. Instead of seeing life as a succession of traumas, a gauntlet of pain that she must endure until her death, she began to entertain the idea that there was a purpose to her life and an unfolding of her destiny that she could anticipate. She would take the necessary steps as best as she could determine, and then wait and watch for signs. Aside from her children, nothing else contained value. Again, Campbell: "The call to adventure . . . signifies that destiny has summoned the hero and transferred his spiritual center of gravity from within the pale of his society to a zone unknown."[7]

> I began to think that I *needed* to have that profound an experience of the light and the healing in order to make the choice to leave my circumstances. The fast life had been very

powerful for me, and the most attractive thing to me at the time. After that, I began to seek out healers of all types. I began to go to conferences and gatherings in order to hear other stories and get more of a sense of what happened to me. I began to read spiritual texts, and I learned massage.

The next years were peaceful ones. Tara had finally regained custody of her children and in addition, she had taken in two runaways. She found employment as the assistant to the president of the Washington State Massage Association, and although the blend of a nascent professional life with family responsibilities was a hectic one, Tara found herself happier than ever. She finally felt a sense of home. She felt lovingly surrounded by the chaos of budding adolescents, and her work as a massage therapist and administrator for the state association seemed to be just the beginning of a true vocation. The isolation of childhood seemed more a distant, almost disconnected, memory, as if it happened to someone else, and she rarely thought of the native heritage that fate had conspired to shield from her. For the most part, these years were a rich and pleasant respite, and Tara didn't feel that much else was needed or required.

THE PARADOX OF THE CALL

Five years after her harrowing illness, Tara was offered two tickets to Hawaii for the Christmas holiday. Having lived most of her life in the northwest, the proposal sounded like a dream, and she would fantasize what it would feel like for her skin to be caressed by an equatorial sun and tropical waters. She could arrange child care, the older kids could help out, and it was a chance to really get away for awhile. Despite the inordinate amount of traveling in both childhood and during her second marriage, she could not remember enjoying a legitimate vacation. This was precisely what she was thinking that steel-gray late autumn afternoon when the stranger appeared. It was an encounter that would change her life more dramatically than any before.

> It was in late November. I was cleaning house—vacuuming the rug—and this man just blipped into my living room. Just appeared there! He was a very short Native American man. There wasn't a great deal of substance to the image. I could see right through him, but he was there. He was bowlegged and stood bent over. He pointed his bony finger at me and, in very broken English, said, "Before the year is out, you will be with me in Taos."

The Call appears in our lives in innumerable ways. As we shall hear in virtually all of these stories, each person experiences it through different senses, for different durations of time, and at varied degrees of intensity. Yet, if we listen closely, we can also detect a similar and compelling structure to the Call that is common to them all. The Call contains two apparently contradictory aspects: On the one hand, the form is bizarre or alien. There is a distinct "otherness" to it, and to its entry into our lives. On the other hand, it is utterly familiar, striking the most intimate of chords, in the deepest portion of our soul, often in the most personally symbolic way. Upon cursory inspection they seem irreconcilable polarities. Joined together, they seem the very archetype of paradox. And yet, this is precisely how the Call functions. The world we are deposited into after the arrival of the Call is not one of easy contrasts, of black and white. Enigmatic by nature, the Call requires us to expand ourselves to embrace both sides if we are to successfully negotiate the journey. As cultural anthropologists and mythologists consistently observe, both the survival of rites of passage as well as success on the quest require that we expand ourselves to enjoin apparent opposites.[8,9]

Except for the light, Tara had never seen something as compelling as the old man. The time and place of the vision were completely ordinary, but his presence and message were anything but.

> I was surprised, to say the least. I wasn't sure if it was true. I'm always very skeptical at first when something unusual happens. I was thinking to myself, *"I don't know if this is real or not, but it's* so *strong. Maybe it was worth checking out."* There was such a powerful sense of calling to him.

At a deeper level, the old man seemed to speak in code, not only to the adult woman before him, but to the virtually orphaned girl she had once been almost thirty years before. For not only had the unexpected appeared as a Native American, it spoke to her about New Mexico, specifically Taos—the only place she and her father consistently lived, the only place that felt like a home after the family fell apart.

> I hadn't been back since I was a child. It was the place that was native to me and closest to my heart. That was Taos.

Having learned her earlier lesson well, Tara realized she still had a choice. The tickets to Hawaii exerted a delightful tug, but the more she reviewed her experience, the more compelling it seemed. And if there was any doubt, it was quickly dispelled upon learning that her boyfriend, to whom she had offered a ticket, declined her invitation to the islands. Unbeknownst to her, he was planning a trip to New Mexico for an appointment at a healing center. It had taken over a year to secure and had just come through.

It was as if bread crumbs were being dropped in the forest to show her the way. Tara felt she had truly received a sacred summons. She wasn't sure if it was synchronicity or just co-incidence, but her lover's reply was enough to convince her to forgo Hawaii. Regrettably at first, Tara gave away her tickets and made plans to visit the adobe pueblos of Taos by the end of the year.

> So before the year was out, literally on the thirtieth of December, we arrived in Taos. Already something deep had been stirred inside me. The day before, as we were driving along US 285, along this piñon forest, I burst into tears. I made Dan stop the car and I ran into the woods and disappeared. Dan must have been wondering a bit about me. It was a pretty new relationship. This was our first trip together! He found me a half hour later on my knees, crying. I was so thankful to be back in New Mexico, to be home.

> We camped out that night, nearly froze to death, because we didn't have much money and I wanted to be at Taos pueblo at dawn. For some reason, I felt I had to be there at sunrise, at the beginning of the day to look for the old man. We were both very excited. We were there all day, and we went from house to house, looked at the people, and wandered around. And at any moment, I thought I would see the man who appeared in my living room. I was sure, if I was here, I'd find him. We wandered and looked all day. Nothing.

They had knocked at virtually every door on the reservation. They were cold and had barely stopped for food. As the shadows lengthened and the thin winter's light began to fade, so too did their spirits. Tara had begun to doubt both her experience and her sanity, and she felt her failure fall awkwardly between herself and Dan.

> I didn't know him real well yet, and by the end of the day, I was feeling very embarrassed. Finally, I said, "It must have been just my imagination." I felt very disappointed and resigned. But just as we were leaving, I noticed a sign in a doorway that we had apparently missed. It was a very little sign. It read, CURIOS scrawled in really poor lettering, almost illegible. I said, "We haven't been here yet. Let's knock, and if he isn't there, then we'll leave and try to forget about the whole thing." So we knocked. Nothing. We knocked again. Again nothing. We knocked a couple of times more. Still nothing.

They turned to walk off the reservation. Tara was downcast, and there seemed nothing that Dan could offer in solace. They were almost out of earshot when suddenly, the old pine door creaked open.

> And there he was! There was the little man I had seen! He stuck his head out, and he cried, "My children! My children! I have been waiting. You have come!" He brought us in. He sat us by the fire and fed us. He sang sacred songs and he told us stories all through the night. It felt like the most important event of my life. There wasn't anything drawing my attention outside of that room. It was clear, through the stories and the songs, that he was opening me to a part of who I was and finally welcoming me into my own family. It was him. It was an amazing confirmation of the vision.
>
> He was a *kasiki,* meaning the head of a kiva. It takes many years to earn that role. He was a legendary hunter in the village. He had the ability to sleep out, without any covers or blankets, even in the coldest winter. If he didn't have any blankets, he would sleep right on the snow. He would also traverse the icy rivers in moccasins. He never mentioned the vision in my house. Indians rarely explain. Things are just

assumed and understood. It was clear, though, he was our "Grandfather."

Dawn approached. It was time to leave. The darkness that surrounded their modest sanctuary had given way to the year's first morning. Grandfather finished singing, and his children were sated. Tara rose and moved to the portal that hours before allowed a passage back to her heritage, and as the piñon door once again creaked open, her feet felt leaden in their reluctance to go.

> As we left he said, "You come back September twenty-ninth next year." I said, "Well, I live in Washington and if it works out, then . . ." And he interrupted me and said it again, more forcefully this time: "You come back September twenty-ninth! You come back!" So it was scheduled! There wasn't much else to say. I knew in my bones he was my spiritual grandfather and that I had to come.

The experience left an afterglow that rendered ordinary reality pale. During the long drive home, she wrestled with herself. Tara wanted only to savor the sweetness of the night. It was a connection she had believed would never happen. Tara once believed that the door to that possibility had closed, and she left the scars to heal as best they could. But Grandfather's songs laid bare those wounds with an exquisite tenderness, and, for a time, Tara felt raw.

> I went home and cried a great deal. There was grief for the many years without that connection. And there was longing—longing to be back at the pueblo and with Grandfather. When we were there, he didn't teach much, no great discourses or anything. His teaching was his utter simplicity and lovingness. He was so gentle with us. It was really the familiarity, feeling a part of my native family, that was so profound.

In the car, Tara sensed she was starting over, as if this were the first day of her life. It was only with discipline that, upon approaching Seattle, she turned her mind to the children and to the particulars of her future. Just as her grandfather's first appearance demanded her presence in Taos, Tara knew that she must return. She chuckled to herself. The question was not only "How?" but "How many?" Tara had a sizable ensemble to think about, and it was important to consider their best interests as well. As powerfully as Tara felt guided, she hesitated making an impulsive move. Tara knew a relocation would require a significant period of adjustment, and she couldn't fathom what that would look like with seven children. But she couldn't afford frequent trips to New Mexico, and aside from the hard-won stability she enjoyed over the past few years, there was no compelling reason *not* to go.

> I decided to go back in September, but I hadn't yet made up my mind to move. I told the children about Grandfather, and about Dan, and our idea that *perhaps,* someday, we might want to consider moving south to Colorado where Dan lived. I agonized about it for a couple of weeks. Every time I would agonize in front of the kids, they would say, "Well, let's go!" You know, life was difficult up there for us, and *they* were difficult up there and they were ready.

Tara spent hours on the phone with Dan. They rekindled the wonder they felt had cradled them in the simple firelit room. They talked of the practicalities involved in moving the children, and of how he would fare as the de facto stepfather. And they talked about each other, for although the bond felt strong, they recognized that the relationship was new for such ambitious plans.

After a few weeks, however, Tara became certain. In pre-

vious years, her decisions would be determined by the desires
of others. It was now time for a change. Somehow, she would
have to trust that if she was touched so profoundly, the children
would benefit as well. Dan sent some money for the trip, and
the rest was funded by selling possessions that remained from
her former marriages.

> The last was a Harry Winston wedding ring. I got just a
> fraction of what it was worth, but in selling it, I ended that
> life. I packed up the children, the dog, cats, and what few
> belongings I could stuff into the cars, and we moved to
> Colorado.

Crestone lies just to the north of the Great Sand Dunes
National Monument, in south-central Colorado. The small town
sits at the end of the San Luis Valley, whose floor dropped to
8,000 feet during the Laramide orogeny, the geologic uplift that
produced the Rocky Mountains over eighteen million years ago.
A stark and spare region, Crestone has only a three-month
growing season and is daily scoured by the dry winds that plunge
from the Sangre de Cristo Mountains to the east. Although it
seems desolate at first glance, there is something quite fertile
about this town. In a community of only 400, there lies a
Carmelite monastery, a Tibetan temple, two Zen priories, a
Subud Muslim worship center, and a Hindu shrine. In recent
years, Crestone has been identified as a sacred spot by practi-
tioners of many faiths, and people throughout the world come
for spiritual practice and guidance. In fact, at times of pilgrimage
in Crestone, it is not clear whether one is standing in the United
States or on the Tibetan plateau.

Dan and Tara chose Crestone for their home. Taos lay only
two hours to the south and their interests had begun to embrace
not only Native American traditions, but those of the East as

well. They learned the austerity of the Zen *sesshin,* felt transported by the devotional practices of Vedanta, and were, in fact, married a few years later by two Tibetan monks with whom they forged a deep and lasting bond. Last but not least, Tara had become an adopted and honored member of her grandfather's family in Taos Pueblo. Her passage was complete. The child who had grown up grasping for validation from white culture had finally been welcomed into her own. There she finally experienced a blessed belonging. Tara learned to rest and revel in the silence of her complete acceptance, and for the first time in her life, she felt whole.

The nature of the unexpected, whether big or small, compels us to question who or what is the principal actor on the stage of our lives. Those I've interviewed on these pages were intelligent and resourceful people, capable of creative thought and purposeful action. Faced with the challenge of providing for themselves and their families, they more than ably did so. Yet during those astonishing moments when people have encountered the unexpected, they sense a power or presence, an intelligence or feeling of love much greater than anything they'd ever known, or known about. This is a hallmark of the Call. These are moments when we discover we are not so much leading, but being led; not claiming our experience, but being claimed by a larger, more fantastic power than we ever imagined.

When living systems—be they single-celled organisms, animal colonies, individuals, families, or multinational organizations—are ready to evolve to the next level of complexity, rigid structures dissolve, boundaries become more permeable, and roles more flexible. These are dynamic transitional periods, where we may be profoundly impacted by external events, and where cherished beliefs and familiar responses to them often prove anachronistic. This was true of Jordan, a physician and research scientist for over fifty years. In the presence of the unexpected, he realized that the wisest recourse was to acknowledge that what was occurring was at least momentarily beyond his control. The Call emerges from a source much deeper or greater than the conscious mind or personal volition. Like a child's first sight of a rainbow, a shooting star, or an evening's storm, it is a time of wonder and awe.

Jordan

THE PHYSICIAN WHO HATED CHURCHES

Jordan is in his mid-seventies. A bespeckled man with gray hair and a closely cropped white mustache and goatee, he is warm and amiable. When he speaks, his deep blue eyes are animated, even mischievous in their sparkle. Jordan has lost much of the British reserve he learned as a young man, and when he spoke of his past, it was with sincerity and candor.

As early as he could remember, Jordan found himself fascinated with the physical world. He spent hours as a child by himself in the fields surrounding Sutton-on-Sea in the northeast county of Lincolnshire, "Lincs" as the locals called it, catching caterpillars and butterflies, frogs and snakes, rabbits and moles—examining creatures of all kinds that were indigenous to the region. Like her neighbors to the east in Holland, the township lay twelve feet below sea level. The sandy fields had to be drained for farming, and the dikes were in constant repair.

Winters were damp and cold, as a bitter east wind would blow off the rough North Sea. Summers offered some respite and were muggy and overcast. During that short season, on the few days that the clouds would part, a hot sunlight would steam the earth and suffuse the wildflowers that blanketed the distant heaths in a pale white light.

Sutton-on-Sea was a small, conservative village, population only 2,000; simple working-class people—dairy farmers and fishermen with deep family roots that stretched back hundreds of years. Jordan's family was poor, but prominent in the town. One uncle was the postmaster, another chairman of the town council, and his father, a respected former captain in the royal flying corps, Britain's precursor to the air force. During World War I, his mother functioned as the town's only vital link to information in the outer world:

> She was only eighteen, but she ran the local post office during the war. She was tough and resourceful, and she was the only person who knew Morse code; the only one who could work the "instrument." She could take coded messages and carry on a conversation at the same time.

Jordan grew up during the unsettled years between the world wars. Sutton had become a small seaside resort and was a shelter from the tumult. Its idle charms allowed the children relative protection from political unrest and afforded the townspeople needed extra income by renting rooms to visitors from Cambridge, Manchester, Leeds, and other cities in northern England.

> The village was a place apart, very little stress, as far as I remember. There was a lot of gossip—social skirmishes and minor scandals—but I had little sense of damage from the first war or postwar repair.

I threw myself into my own studies: Einstein's relativity, organic chemistry, biology, and basic physics, so by the time I was fourteen, I was building cathode ray tubes, neon signs, and vacuum pumps by myself. I paid no attention to the papers or the talk of a new war. I was totally unaware of political realities. I thought Hitler was of no account, and when England declared war, I thought it ludicrous. I was building X-ray machines, but I still knew nothing about life.

The survival of his country and the very future of Europe were doubtful, but the direction of Jordan's career path was clear, even in childhood. His fascination with the physical world superseded all other interests. It became his laboratory, and because he spent most of his time alone, his primary companion.

I was just a curious little boy who liked to do experiments. I really couldn't understand why everyone else didn't feel the same way. To me, it felt like the only really interesting thing to do was to find out what the world was made of and how everything worked. I got my first chemistry set before I could read.

In those youthful days Jordan learned the perception and persistence that formed the style with which he continued his science and, eventually, his medical training. And although the subject of his investigations became more formal as he grew, the essential experience remained the same.

I wasn't a routine scientist. In fact, I actually never learned about the scientific method until after I retired and I was helping a friend with a night course she was taking. For me, it was much more common sense—absorbing a lot of facts about a specific subject, really locating my mind with it, and trying to figure out what was happening and then trying to devise an experiment that would sort of trap the information and show it was so.

Jordan developed the capacity for an almost single-minded engagement in his studies, and despite the portentous geo-political shadow that beclouded Great Britain, he continued to develop as one of the country's most promising young scientists. By this time, however, a national fervor had swept England, and every able-bodied man and woman was expected to contribute to the war effort. As if to emphasize the need, Lincolnshire, historically shielded from conflict, had become the target of sporadic but terrifying Nazi air raids. The town was ordered black after sundown and townspeople spent nights in fear. Young men and women everywhere were leaving the farms to volunteer for service. Already grateful to the government for subsidizing his medical studies, Jordan saw military service as the patriotic way to repay his debt.

> By the time I finished medical training, all I wanted was to get into a uniform. One of my cousins was a parachutist, another a spitfire pilot, and a third a tank commander. When I was home, I served in the home guard, a ragged militia forged by each township. I would keep watch for German Panzers in a slit trench with a shotgun! It was a joke. We had no rifles or machine guns, and if there *were* a fight, we'd be hopelessly overmatched.

> I finished medical school in 1943, when I was twenty-two, and immediately enlisted. I spent six months in the British navy as a surgeon lieutenant with the North Atlantic Convoys. I was pretty scared, but not so much of drown-ing—it *is* one of the most treacherous bodies of water in the world—but of having to do some big-deal operation that I had, as yet, never done. On my first leave, I went to practice surgery at a local hospital—hernias, appendixes, things like that. After that, I felt much better.

As England began her difficult repair from the war, Jordan opened a modest private practice in general medicine, hoping to earn some money for his more enduring interest, a post-doctoral fellowship in biochemistry at Cambridge. It was the top department in the country, and once accepted, Jordan continued to apply the spirit of inquiry that had become both play and second nature to him. His success there was followed with an appointment to a position at the National Institute for Medical Research, England's equivalent to the National Institute of Health. After some years, he emigrated to Canada, to undertake advanced training in virology at the University of British Columbia. In 1958, he was appointed the director of virology for the New York State Department of Health, a position he kept for almost thirty years until he retired.

> That's where I met Lois. She was a lab tech in my department. I was unhappily married, but I didn't believe in divorce. When Lois and I fell in love with each other, I went through a lot of guilt and a lot of grief in facing the fact that I had to make a decision. It took me four years before giving myself permission to get divorced and eight years more to come around to marrying again. I wish I had done it earlier.

Jordan began to awaken from a slumber. Until he met Lois, his marriage had been circumscribed by his studies and shaped by the form and image of marriages of the seaside villages in England. He was still a relatively inexperienced young man, and although his first wife and he were loyal and dutiful toward one another, he questioned whether he had actually ever been in love. In Lois, Jordan met a colleague and an intellectual equal, but also someone with whom he could explore a passionate life of wider interests—travel and culture—and for the first time, true intimacy.

> Ours was a very close mental molding—her personality with mine. We spent many hours in the lab together, wrote papers

together, skied together, and although we also had separate
interests and we got on each other's nerves from time to
time, we seemed to match on many levels. Quite naturally,
what was important to her was to me, and vice versa. We
both learned to play musical instruments—I'd play the oboe
and she the flute, and that was a good simile for what it was
like to be together: some beautiful interaction between the
two that you don't get solo. We were married for thirty-
five years.

As a child and young adult, Jordan had come to accept
solitude. His mother had died when he was ten, and his father
rarely joined him in exploration and play. But Lois pierced his
isolation and nudged him into a more relational world. When
life offered its challenges, Jordan and Lois confronted them with
a togetherness he had never known. Into this warmth, they
adopted two girls from India and settled in a suburb of Albany
to raise them. Nearly twelve years passed. Jordan and Lois continued working together, and their family flourished. They grew
to be rich with friends, extended family, intellectual challenges,
and in their love for each other and their children. Then, suddenly, came the diagnosis.

When we realized Lois had cancer, I was the one to tell her.
It felt like someone else was speaking. Her prognosis was
very poor and the doctors felt she had less than a year to
live. I didn't know what I was going to say to her, or how,
but I heard myself say, "If you die, I shan't want to live."

It was some kind of dependency in a way, but it also summed
up how important she was to me. The change in me was
remarkable that year. I became very unselfish. I learned to
put myself aside and let her be most important. In the hospice, I would sleep on the floor, or she would pat the bed

to indicate she wanted me to hold her through the night. I would have gladly taken the cancer for her if I could have.

Lois and Jordan were unwilling to be passive and let fate dictate their remaining time together. They decided to travel. Their girls were in late adolescence and would be comfortable with friends. The break from the daily stress of their mother's decline would be welcome. After a few weeks, they would follow, so the family could be together. Jordan and Lois bought a motor home and drove to Florida, anticipating lazy days by the warm water, soft, radiant sunsets, and a timelessness that would help them forget. They would create a world of their own, a reality apart, and simply surround themselves with each other. They would keep death at bay, and they would steal time. Shortly after their arrival, however, their dreams were deflated. Doctors discovered that the tumors metastasized more quickly than they predicted, and Lois had progressively more difficulty breathing. They had hoped for months together in the South, but the reality was different. After a few weeks, realizing her time was near, they flew home.

I knew if we stayed much longer, she wouldn't be well enough to get back home. We went to the local hospice, St. Peter's, a place she felt safe, and they were able to aid her breathing and eliminate her pain.

The day she died, less than a month after getting back from Florida, she actually felt a lot better. She was perky and cheerful and was scheduled to go home the following day. This kind of interval is common with dying people. But, later that evening, she complained her legs were cold, and blankets didn't seem to help. She was having trouble breathing, so I had the nurse give her some morphine. It was a hard decision to make. I knew it would probably hasten her death a bit, and I would prefer she wouldn't die so fast and that we could talk. On the other hand, she was frightened, and I knew this would help her relax. Pretty soon, I could find no pulse . . . and no blood pressure, and I knew. I closed her eyes. They were a very deep blue.

Jordan sat with the woman with whom he had been joined for over three decades. The physician in him was composed, even clinical. He had known death: his mother when he was a child, a number of relatives in the war, and the countless patients for whom he was powerless. From his early adventures in the garden, through his postgraduate training, the biologist in him knew he was simply witnessing the endless cycle of births and deaths that occur in nature millions of times each day. But, as a husband, he sat at her side unbelieving. He could not comprehend the finality of what had just occurred.

> I wanted to stay there the night with her. Not in a morbid way, but I really needed time to get used to the idea that she was no longer alive. I cut off a lock of her hair. I still have it in my wallet. I wanted some little piece of her to keep. I still identified her body as her and it took a while to feel it wasn't her anymore. Outside I looked calm, but inside I felt deep anguish. We hadn't been out of each other's company for even an hour during the last months. At that moment, I really would have liked to have gone with her.

The loss of a spouse constitutes one of the greatest stresses of our lives. Nearly eight million Americans experience the death of a nuclear family member each year, and reports estimate that as a consequence there are more than 800,000 new widows and widowers.[10]

The classic writings in psychology recognize mourning as the essential response to loss.[11] When allowed to progress unimpeded, mourning provides a time outside of time for reflection, rest, and repair. Interactions with family, friends, and neighbors are often deeper, more soulful, and in that way, the community may support and encourage the process of recovery. Grieving allows a psychological space for the complex layering of remembering and letting go; of savoring the past, even clinging to our loved ones (and thereby keeping them alive for a while longer), while slowly, painfully beginning to unwind the attachments and dependencies created over so many years. For when mourning is examined more closely, it involves not only the loss of someone we love, but of a large part of ourselves—our identity as a person connected to someone else and the life that engendered. As Judith Viorst, author of the exceptionally lucid work *Necessary Losses*, states:

> For the changes in our bodies redefine us. The events of our personal history redefine us. The ways that others perceive us redefine us. And at several points in our life we will have to relinquish a former self-image and move on.[12]

When allowed its natural course, grieving ushers the beginning of healing. But when the normal process of mourning is interrupted, we can become stuck, fixated at the point of the loss, and unable either to grieve fully or to move on. Typically, such complicated or incomplete mourning results in feelings of unremitting grief, anxiety, guilt, helplessness, and great fatigue.

Jordan needed time to rest and to absorb the enormous change that had befallen him. But Lois's death was not his loss alone. His daughters, now fifteen and eighteen, were also having difficulty. In response to the tragedy, the younger became contentious and promiscuous, and the older, withdrawn and angry. The girls had suffered a grave loss, but to compound matters, they felt their father's anguish and it frightened them. As if to ensure against losing another parent, a thought too terrifying to express directly, they began to require greater proximity of him—to monitor their activities and to pay closer attention to their behavior and moods, however unappealing.

The younger one began to get into loads of trouble. She became defiant and, uncharacteristically, began to act out. She began chasing boys, stealing things, even distributing our house keys to friends and acquaintances. At one point, I had to put a deadbolt on my bedroom door! The older became very sullen. She was the closer one to Lois. She had been furious at her for being ill, once even lunging at her in a rage during the final days. She felt that her mother was deserting her. Life was pretty difficult for a while. I was pretty worn down by it. I would wake with the anxiety that not only was Lois dead, but that the rest of my family was falling apart.

The medical crisis that had begun with Lois spawned emotional concussions that shattered the family. Resigned, Jordan realized that the rest he so dearly needed was not yet possible. He had become a parent in middle age, and now in his late sixties, he felt exhausted, depressed, and numb. The rich and full family life that he and Lois had created seemed ground to an incomprehensible halt, and for the first time, Jordan wondered whether he had the patience, wisdom, and fortitude to reverse the fall.

I felt so low. I didn't have my normal gumption. I had purchased a copy of *Final Exit*, to see what they'd recommend, but I didn't take any steps. I threw away all our pills because I didn't want to fall prey to a moment of weakness.

One morning, I was sitting at the kitchen table, feeling poorly, realizing that I needed help. I decided to call an old friend, one who I hadn't spoken to in a while. Max's wife had died three years previously and I wanted to ask him how he handled it. Hints and advice. He suggested we go on an Elderhostel to Arizona, six weeks hence. I once traveled around the world by myself, but now my energy was so low, and I really wondered whether I would have the strength to go.

Despite reservations, Jordan committed to the trip and discovered that for the first time since Lois's death, he actually looked forward to something. The tour, an exploration of the southwest for elders, would reunite him with an old friend, now one of similar circumstance. It would give him a chance to speak candidly about his grief and allow some time away from the chaos of the family. As the junket began, Jordan felt something of his old self returning.

It was a wonderful respite. I was enjoying myself. I wasn't particularly feeling much grief on the trip. I was feeling upbeat. Just what I needed. Of course, there were moments of missing Lois, but this was the first time since her death that I was actually having a good time.

Toward the end of the trip, I think it was Friday, we were scheduled to visit the local zoo. We were on a bus, and it veered off on a detour; a side dirt road that went to an old church—San Xavier del Bac. I was kind of pissed off because I didn't want to do that. As we all got out, I jokingly said, "Well there's the church, now you've seen it, now let's get back on the bus." That was my frame of mind, but there was really nothing else I could do but go along. I could never have anticipated how powerful the next few minutes would be.

In Greek, the word *mimesis* connotes an experience of merging with one's world in order to know it. It is somatic, poetic, even erotic,[13] and describes a quality of union with the nodal events of our lives that yields understanding long before rational comprehension. Virtually instant, it occurs through a near-total identification with the event, where boundaries between the experience and the experiencer become blurred and diffuse. Time becomes elastic but also compressed into a supercharged moment. In this altered state, people become uncommonly sensitive. Visual, auditory, and kinesthetic experiences occur that would normally seem impossible. Meaning is conveyed, but not through normal communication. It is immediate and "visceral." For many, the import of the event and the precise reason for its entry into a person's life are instantly realized. Jordan's experience in the church provides a powerful example of "visceral knowing," and his description takes us to the very heart of the experience of being deeply and profoundly moved.

> It seemed like a waste of time. I had no interest in Catholic churches and I felt cheated out of the couple of hours that we could have spent at the zoo. I was brought up a narrow-minded Methodist in Lincolnshire. My father was a lay preacher, and I used to be on the pulpit with him when he spoke. That gave me more than a bit of confusion as to how he was connected to God.

Jordan's state of mind approaching the church was significant in two ways. First, he was actually enjoying himself on the trip. This was a great relief, as it was the first time he felt his despair lift since Lois had died. He wasn't hoping for a healing experience, nor was he even thinking about it. Second, he greeted the possibility of exploring the church with antipathy. It seemed like a poor choice for a vacation activity, and he was dubious of its emotional, spiritual, or cultural relevance to him. Only with reluctance did he consent to enter. He didn't know that as he strained to open the church's massive antique door, he stood at the threshold of a passage—to a momentous meeting and toward his rebirth.

> I was surprised how much I liked it . . . warm, cozy, even friendly feeling. I was quite amazed I was so taken. Normally I dislike Catholic churches as too ornate. There were rows of candles burning for loved ones—with notes on them like, "Jesus, please take care of my Anna. Make her well." I started thinking of the people here who were probably a lot worse off than I was. I began to feel a lot of empathy and caring for them.
>
> Just at that moment, I felt a warmth in the back of my head and in my chest, as if someone were peering at me from behind, and with it came a conviction that some important person had just come into the church. I thought it must have been a local bishop, and he had come in and was looking at me. I turned around to see who it was, but there was no one there. I looked elsewhere, but still saw nobody, and then, it's a little hard to describe, came a feeling of knowing that *someone* was in the church. It grew in intensity and became enormously strong—ten times, a thousand times, a million times stronger . . . and then I had a sense of total certainty. It seemed even stronger than the fact that *I* was in the church.
>
> I started to cry. I became filled with ecstasy, for I knew, at that moment, Lois was there. The information seemed to be beamed into the back of my head and continued to escalate. I felt total ecstasy—an orgasm of the heart—and I felt in my chest a supreme happiness. I cried out in joy. I remember thinking that this was so good, I was never going to leave the church. They would have to drag me out!

Jordan had always been a passionate man, but guided by typical English restraint, his expression of passion was formal and muted. When he exclaimed in heartfelt joy, his composure dissolved and he surrendered. Knees buckling, he fell onto a pew. The power of the event was indisputable, and at the same time, its meaning seemed immediately and undeniably clear.

> It was just solid knowledge, and it seemed to be coming into my head from the outside and not the slightest degree arising from inside me. Again, I had not wanted to go into the church and had no intention of something like this happening. Sitting on a pew, I knew three things with absolute certainty: One, that Lois was there and I was with her. Two, that she was in a state of extreme happiness. And three, that some very important superior being was there, looking after her. It was as certain as the fact that I was in the church and sitting on a pew. I can't say how long it was—perhaps ten minutes, maybe more. I just stayed there absorbing this delicious feeling that I was with her and she was all right. I felt totally happy and utterly safe. It was marvelous.

Jordan's training had taught him to monitor the progression of his thoughts as he worked a problem to its scientific conclusion. Hypotheses would arise and then be confirmed or discarded based on logic and sound experimental design. As a result, he would know how or why something worked, and then could proceed accordingly. The experience in the church, however, introduced Jordan to a different kind of knowing. It hadn't come from intellectual understanding of the event, but from a complete absorption and merging with it. No longer a scientist distanced from nature in order to understand it, Jordan was both subject and witness, the knower and the known. And into this transported state, meaning effortlessly arose: Lois was well and happy wherever she was, and that she had come to let him know.

After ten minutes or so, Jordan slowly rose to leave. Fa-

tigued, he also noticed a state of well-being that moved with
him toward the door.

> I began to feel slightly used up; it was requiring energy to
> continue to feel this good and I was beginning to try to hold
> on to it, rather than just experience it. I realized that I was
> satisfied and I could let it go. I was happy, and I had enough,
> like after a meal. I felt it was time to go. I put some money
> in the box, and passed through the door.

When Jordan walked from the soft light and muffled tones
of the church, into the harsh sun of the Arizona afternoon, he
felt the charge begin to fade. There was still a palpable feeling
of expansion, but rather than surrounding and enveloping him,
he felt it settle within him. Jordan's first impulse was to find
his friend and describe what occurred in great detail. What
happened next provides an excellent illustration of the difficulty
returning to "normal" life after an experience of the unexpected. Jordan found himself in a curious territory—out of sync
and separate.

> Max was standing just outside, looking up at the cornices of
> the church. He was a retired architect and that was usually
> the first thing that drew his attention wherever we went. I
> ran to him and yelled, "Max! I need to tell you about an
> amazing thing that happened to me inside the church!" And
> he said, not really paying attention, "Really, uh-huh. I want
> you to look at this design." So, I didn't bother to tell him,
> since he wasn't listening. Then a priest came out, and I went
> over, intending to tell him that something very remarkable
> just happened to me in his church, but just as I approached,
> a young girl ran up to him, and he turned and they began
> talking very animatedly. I wrote him a letter later and gave
> a donation, but I never got a response.

The aftereffects of Jordan's union with Lois lasted for some time. Long after he returned from his vacation, Jordan continued to feel joy and delight, knowing that Lois was happy, and she had been able to communicate with him. Nearly a decade since her passing, their love and that experience continue to nourish him.

> Sometimes I have a thought about her and there is a pang of grief. Mostly, these days, it turns into a feeling of joy. Grief seems to start with an almost unbearable pain for me, and then it becomes less so, and then, with a feeling like I had in the church, it turns to happiness.

The fullness of their lives together, combined with the unexpected, yielded a remarkable experience. Conjoined in a profound dialectic, Jordan noticed that his pain would dissolve into ecstasy and ecstasy could be savored by not avoiding the pain. Although Lois's passing would leave an indelible hole in his heart, that heart would still function and, further, be capable of a robust emotional life.

> I won't say I don't miss Lois. I don't want her dead. But the feelings that used to be so painful are now connected with exquisite happiness. If I feel grief now, and when I almost feel like crying, if I wait a bit, I know now that it will become an ecstatic feeling of joy.

To the grieving husband of thirty-five years, the experience in the church provided a completion. For the scientist, it inspired an unexpected rebirth.

Jordan's adventure seemed to violate nearly every aspect of the traditional scientific worldview. A dead woman returns to communicate. There was no form to see, but the encounter was tangible. Further, the meaning of the event was clear, although no conventional discourse took place. These experiences were just too juicy to leave alone, and for the first time, since Lois's decline, Jordan felt inspired again.

> I was left with the conundrum that either I had a hallucination, which I've never had before or since, or *something* happened. If I had to bet, I'd unhesitatingly place my money on the proposition that something real happened and it came from outside me.

> It started me on a quest. After nearly fifty years, my scientific curiosity stopped being focused on things—viruses, electricity, whatever—and switched to the more spiritual, metaphysical, mystical arena. I've been to a lot of conferences and workshops, and I've read one hundred or so books on all aspects of spiritual search. I've even gone to Princeton University to participate in experiments there on how human consciousness seems to affect the operation of highly sophisticated computer equipment. So I've totally moved out from hard science in the laboratory to, hopefully, hard but more nebulous research on more spiritual levels. It's very exciting. A total shift for me. I'm becoming connected to something far bigger than me.

From where does the Call come? Is it a communication divinely sent, orchestrated in God's infinite wisdom to propel us beyond ego-centered identifications? Or is it a message in code that emanates from a place so deep within the unconscious that we have little awareness of it?[14] As we close this chapter, the question of source must be addressed. We might agree that Rebecca had lamentably found herself in the middle of a terrible storm. It was certainly bad fortune, but was it divinely sent? To her credit, she was able to call upon the capacity of heart and mind to find meaning in the storm and begin to give her life a new direction. Her experience could simply serve to reinforce the belief that human beings have a near-infinite ability to discover meaning in adversity. And Christopher? Noticing the juxtaposition of images against the night sky seems a benign though meaningful event that pointed toward his future. Nothing too unusual there. But what about the voice? Some might say it was an emanation from his unconscious, responding to hesitation or fear. But could it have truly been the voice of God? And then there is Tara. Many first-person accounts seem to demonstrate that the near-death experience is, in itself, an altered state of consciousness. It is possible that experiences within this state reflect our mind's often-unused ability to discern the true nature of and purpose for our lives. Perhaps the extreme physiological state of the body further prompts the psyche toward an unusual lucidity, stretching thought processes beyond conventional modes. But how does that explain the appearance of the old man, and Tara's uncanny encounter with him months later? And finally, how can we understand *his* recognition of *her* when he opened the door?

Even though I have spent my entire adult life in the field of psychology, I continue to be astonished that, to date, so few schools of psychological thought have even begun to address these questions.[15] As opposed to his mentor, Sigmund Freud, the Swiss analyst Carl Jung was continually drawn to the boundary between psychological and spiritual phenomena. Whereas Freud attempted to interpret most experiences in terms of a personal unconscious—a reservoir of repressed memory and suppressed sexual desire—Jung grew to believe that the source of our dreams and fantasy was vastly deeper and broader in its scope than we ever imagined. As we descend beneath the personal unconscious, he theorized, we enter a treasure trove of symbols, legends, and archetypal energies that, rather than being the sole possession of one individual, forms, as noted analyst

Marion Woodman described, "the great underground river" that connects all humankind across continents and across time, through meaning.

But even an innovative psychological explorer such as Jung could never uncategorically state that *all* external events are inspired by the workings of the psyche.[16] And even if we admit that we cannot definitively prove an event to be either internally produced or divinely sent, we are not poorer for our indecision.

Those I have interviewed for this book have had to wrestle with these same questions. And despite the differences in the individual details, they all shared a similar response. Those who successfully negotiated the quest did not wait for an answer about the Call's source before responding to it. Each may have had a theory about its origin (and many would never have thought to name a supernatural cause), but all recognized its importance and the probability that it conveyed a critical message about their lives. They let the event truly sink in, and they allowed themselves to descend into the inevitable period of separation that followed.[17] This began the incubation period and the search for meaning.

So we are left with the essential human quandary: to hear or not hear, to act or not act. Ultimately, it is one's *readiness* to heed the Call that is most essential at this stage. It is in this choice that our lives take on meaning. For as the esteemed Talmudist and Rabbi Adin Steinsaltz has noted: "Sometimes the only thing to be learned is this: When the Call comes, Jump!"[18]

THREE

THE INCUBATION

THE CALL awakens us. In a single stroke, we are cleaved from the ordinary. Something has changed. We do not return to "normal." It seems folly to try to retrace our steps, and it is difficult to go back. Activities and relationships that had been the primary object of attention (and often, affection) recede in importance, as the compelling mystery of the Call becomes our preoccupation.

The first reaction to the Call is a palpable sense of separation, which is the psyche's essential (and not always comfortable) response. The unexpected poses a profound challenge to the psyche, and a time apart—a distanced posture—becomes necessary to allow for the stretching, even the collapse, of old beliefs and attitudes.

Interestingly, the experience of separation is not one commonly understood in traditional psychology. Too often, this time of withdrawal, of distraction from the everyday, and even of depression has been construed as pathology and understood as an emotional or cognitive malady that must be addressed through a detailed examination of one's history, therapy, or medication. On the surface, this way of thinking seems to make sense. A person seems to be in pain, and psychotherapy may very well be helpful. But it misses the broader context that reveals the sequence and pattern of our passages. To gain that broader context, we must move beyond a psychological perspective, to a cultural one.

For nearly one hundred years, anthropologists have recognized the separation phase in passage rituals throughout the world.[1] In many tribal cultures, the unexpected plays an important part of ritual life. Village elders, shamans, and medicine women have intentionally used surprise, sometimes even terror, to usher in the separation phase:

- In the depth of night, novices are brought from their homes to live in a hut or behind stone walls erected beyond the bounds of the village.
- Initiates are removed to the edge of a forest. Their clothes are taken from them, their faces painted the color of the earth, and they are sent on a solitary journey.
- In some central African clans, a raid is staged by tribesmen disguised as marauders. At night, they steal into family huts and kidnap the young males, while the mothers, startled awake, fight with futility for their rescue. The sons are carried off into the darkness hearing the cries and screams of their families behind them. Although the mothers may be familiar with the ritual, their sons are not, and this first stage of separation is terrifying.

In other communities, odd and disturbing events function to foreshadow the beginning of a passage. Shamanic cultures, for instance, believe that initiations often take the form of a sudden illness,[2] surviving a grave accident,[3] or displaying unusual behavior.[4] Many indigenous groups seem to understand that although the separation phase entails leaving familiar contexts, at its most basic, it marks the dissolution of one's very identity.

Separation actually gives birth to the next two stages of the process: Incubation and the Search for Meaning—both of which are inextricably intertwined. For some people, as we shall hear, the meaning of the event becomes immediately apparent during the moments of the Call. They are propelled into this world apart, to undertake deeper contemplation and to allow for the dialogue to continue. For others, meaning approaches more slowly.[5] Nevertheless, in order for meaning to incubate, the Call moves people into an altered time and place, and they feel oddly alienated from everyday life. Incubation and the Search for Meaning are designed to address the profound questions: What is the message here? Who am I now? What kind of world is this that such a thing can happen?

As mentioned before, there are both active and passive components to transformation. Experiencing the Call is the passive component of the journey of awakening. Whatever its source, an unknown place within the psyche or some intelligence or divinity, we must *be receptive* and *allow* the event to transpire to completion. There is no avoiding it.

The Incubation stage, on the other hand, functions as its active albeit subtle counterpart. But this is not activity in the usual sense. In Incubation, one does not respond immediately with a concrete decision—for instance, to become a lawyer or doctor, move across the country, or marry a particular person. Instead, one surrenders to the separation and Incubation stage that follows with as little grasping, clinging, or bemoaning the loss of what used to be as possible.[6] For some, this world is odd, mysterious, and strange. For others, the feelings run darker, and experiences of the long night—hopelessness, despair, and loss of faith—are common.[7]

In addition, one must recognize that the Call has meaning. At this point in the journey, it is not even important to understand that meaning precisely. This involves a leap of faith: that this event, coming at this point in time, contains crucial significance for who I am now, and for who or what I am to become in the future. This is a powerful, life-transforming posture—a position taken, without adequate proof, but in the adhering, made all the more compelling. For that is the nature of any authentic journey. We become committed to the quest, though the outcome is unknown and even its success never guaranteed. As St. Paul defines faith: "the substance of things hoped for, the evidence of things not seen."[8]

Brooke

THE STAFF OF LIFE

I'm a concert flutist. My career was dying. I was sitting by this large boulder in the backyard—I called it my "thinking stone"—and for the first time since I was really little, I asked God to help me. I said, "Send me a friend and don't let the music die."

Brooke was no stranger to pressure. Since the age of nine, she had been winning music competitions, first locally, then nationally and internationally. She had performed as a soloist on the stages of Carnegie Hall and Lincoln Center, and she had studied with some of the great flutists and performed under some of the most notable conductors in the world. During the most trying times, times of isolation and family discord, she could retreat into the rarefied air of technique and tone, as music was her confidant, her confessor, and her sanctuary. But at the end of a fifteen-year marriage, she found herself depleted and disconnected from her sacred refuge. Brooke was exhausted, and she contemplated ending her life.

> After a lifetime of practice, I hadn't played for over a year; no scales, arpeggios, nothing. My marriage had come apart, and I was depressed and confused. The economic pressures were incredibly intense, and the kids were extremely unhappy and demanding, and wanting my attention nearly all the time. I was trying to finish a book on practice and music education, but was getting no help from my husband. He refused to continue therapy because it was too painful to look at himself, and all I felt was this terrible, terrible sorrow. I knew it was over. I truly had one foot in and one out of this world. I felt like it wasn't worth living, and the only reason I wouldn't kill myself was the children. I was wasting away.

Brooke had always applied a robust optimism to her daily life. Whether practicing études or performing, telling stories after dinner, or collecting neighborhood children for simplified productions of Shakespeare, she believed that each moment, no matter how ordinary, brought the possibility of an encounter with the muse. She applied an indelible creativity to even the smallest task and the most numbing routine. Her enthusiasm was infectious, and friends and family would flock to her to be in an atmosphere of talent, wonder, and self-discovery. For quite a long time, she was able to weather the tension between the richness of that life and the poverty of her marriage, but eventually, the disparity grew too difficult to endure.

One evening, Brooke and her husband decided to see a movie—one of a number of attempts to bring enjoyment back into the marriage or, at the very least, secure some respite from the strain. Sitting in a local bistro later that night, however, the silence and hopelessness once again surrounded them. It was painful, but clear that the marriage had died. Brooke could sense that a portion of her had perished as well.

Brooke's hands are in constant motion as she speaks—to evoke a feeling or emphasize a point—as if she is sculpting the air. After four decades of playing the flute, it seems natural that hands and voice coordinate in almost every conceivable expression. A forty-five-year-old woman with straight jet-black hair and olive-shaped, deep brown eyes, her face flushed with emotion as she began to tell of the thunderbolt that suddenly entered her life.

> After the movie, we sat in a French café, at a little, black, shiny table. We were just staring off into space, not talking. Through the sound system, I noticed this astonishingly beautiful music. It was so innocent. I was heartstruck by it. Suddenly, there was an explosion in my chest, and then a crushing physical sensation. It felt like a bolt of lightning just hit me. It knocked the wind out of me. My chest felt like it was on fire, and I couldn't breathe. Next, everything in the room just disappeared—the patrons, the countertops, the coffee and pastries. I was in some completely altered space.

The music quietly floated through the café. At first, it seemed the most benign of scenes. It is probable that no one else even took notice. But the notes, like a serpent searching for its prey, wound their way through the air and struck Brooke. The gravity of the evening instantly dissolved, and she was given a sign.

> In the air in front of me, I could see music written out on staff paper, floating in the room; black notes dancing on white paper slightly above and in front of me. It was the

music [that was playing] in the café, and I was seeing it appear, at the same moment I was hearing it. It was magical. Then I noticed that there was a gray line, a marker line running through the upper register, and somehow I knew it was a flute part. Then suddenly I realized, *That's my flute part!* I had this sense of absolute certainty.

Deep within the silence of her despair, Brooke had received a Call. In the language that spoke most deeply to her—musical notation—the vision inscribed her signature on an image of the future. However cryptic, Brooke knew that it represented the possibility of her liberation. Invisible to everyone else, the event was so powerful that she awoke from the trance of her depression, and a ray of hope entered.

If the Call is the most obviously powerful event in the Stages of Transformation, the Incubation period may be perhaps the most fascinating. What do people do after the unexpected has so impacted one's world? How do they relate to something so fantastic? Do they talk with others, or do they harbor their secret? Do they seek out community or become private? Do they search for understanding or wait?

Incubation is a time, or rather a "time-out," when the aftershocks of the event continue to be felt and before major decisions and big changes are made. It is a period when one's psyche must stretch in order to accommodate what has transpired and when people attempt to embrace a larger sense of the possible. The word "liminal" (from the Latin, *limin,* meaning "threshold") is often used to describe this period of ambiguity and intentional withdrawal. The normal criteria with which we judge ourselves and evaluate our circumstances must be discarded. Disorientation and aloneness are predominant as people attempt to make sense of and respond to the calling they've received. Behavior seems eccentric and is frequently misunderstood by family and friends. It is as though one has passed through a portal that has rendered him or her invisible. As when Jesus said, "I am not of this world," a spiritual person—in this sense, someone having had a profound experience of another realm—has become separate from the ordinary world and ordinary consciousness. Their faces may be recognizable, but their hearts and minds remain out of reach.

The Incubation period is infused with esoteric (but deeply personal) symbolism and its own arcane language, and all people have to follow are the highly subjective signs and signals that emerge from deep within. For a time, we become lost, "lost enough," in the words of Robert Frost, "to find yourself."

Brooke's experience typifies both the esoteric character of Incubation and the necessity of maintaining the conviction that, despite an abundance of reasons for doubt, the journey contains meaning. Her story is paralleled by two well-known scenes— one from popular culture and one from the Bible. In the classic movie *Close Encounters of the Third Kind*, we find Roy (Richard Dreyfuss) attempting to understand his encounter with a spaceship. Something plagues him. Not only has it been difficult to convince his family of the event, but he is haunted by the sense that he was given a message. Faint and cryptic, the shape of a tower is all he has to guide him. Here, the isolation of the Incubation period is magnificently portrayed: No one seems to understand. Roy has been fired from his job, and rebuked by his wife, who, fearful, piles the children into the car and leaves him. His attempts to explain what he feels only reinforce the separateness.

Perpetually preoccupied, Roy despairs the apparent loss of his sanity and at the same time is singularly obsessed with replicating the tower's form using whatever mutable medium that lies before him—the shaving cream in the bathroom, the clay from his son's train set, or the mashed potatoes at the dinner table. Two or three times, he is heard muttering to himself, "I know this *means* something! It's *important!*" Finally, in one unforgettable scene, he has replicated the tower from mud and garbage, in the center of his living room, with apparent disregard for the furnishings. (Here we can see how the liminal pays little heed to the accoutrements of social convention.) Dreyfuss's character throws himself on the tower, buries his body deep into the dirt to carve a shape that he only faintly remembers. There is no dialogue, but we witness the frenzy of his search and the desperate need that this daft act will render tangible what has been evanescent, and that in doing so, he will begin to make sense of the encounter he had that night on the highway. Finally, covered with mud,[9] he re-creates a tottering mass of upthrusting redrock, volcanic tubes along its spines, and flattened at the top. Breathless, he examines the mountain. At first, it makes no sense. His shoulders slump and resignation begins to encroach. He is both pacing around the tower and on the phone with his wife, pleading for a second chance, declaring that he will surrender his obsession and return to normal. But at that very moment, just when he is about to abandon hope that his fixation meant anything at all, a news report flashes on the television showing a geologic formation in the background that, by now, he recognizes so well. It is Devil's Tower in Wyoming, and Roy realizes that he *was* given a sign—the location of the next encounter. The pieces finally fit together. He hasn't gone mad. Every viewer can revel in Roy's mud-caked triumph.

We can see that Roy had no choice. The ordinary world

offered no formula with which to extract the experience from the recesses of his memory. At the same time, whatever had happened to him was too powerful to ignore. In the Incubation phase, a gut feeling, a faint image, an impulse to go one step further are the only guides we have. Roy simply had to believe that his search had meaning.

In a very different time and place, the Bible tells us of Mary's encounter with the angel Gabriel. Mary, betrothed to Joseph, is told, "Hail, O favored one, the Lord is with you!"[10] Gabriel tells her that she will bear a son named Jesus and that he will be the "Son of the Most High"[11]; "of his kingdom, there will be no end."[12] Now Mary has two problems with this: First, she is a virgin, and second, she is not yet married. Again, the unexpected has little respect for propriety or social convention. The thunderbolt does not consider the style of architecture when it strikes. Gabriel offers proof to the disconcerted Mary, by prophesying that her kinswoman, Elizabeth, who has been infertile, will also give birth. The appearance of an angel along with the prophesies are earthshaking to Mary. Although confused, she surrenders, and declares: "Behold, I am the handmaid of the Lord; let it be to me according to your word."[13] Again, acknowledging the call and recognizing its power are the first steps of the passage.

The Incubation phase is filled with odd occurrences and magical encounters. Visions may continue to appear, and more voices may be heard; subtler variations of the initial calling may repeat itself to move one along the pathless path. The vagaries of the Incubation can sorely test our confidence and resolve, but those who successfully negotiate this period continue to believe two things: There *is* meaning and purpose to the quest, despite how strange it seems, and that they remain connected to a deeper spirit or higher intelligence that, however oblique, is guiding them.

Mary's initial response to her conversation with Gabriel was to leave Nazareth for a time. The separation commences. She "went with haste into the hill country"[14] to give Elizabeth the news. The Bible tells us that when Elizabeth heard Mary's story, a child "leapt into her womb,"[15] and she too was filled with the Holy Spirit.[16] Elizabeth actually feels the baby stir within her, and in one of the most moving passages of the tale, praises Mary. Interestingly, Mary is glorified, not for bearing the son of God, but for trusting the Call. Elizabeth cries: "Blessed is she who believed that there would be a fulfillment of what was spoken to her from the Lord,"[17] to which Mary replies with the ecstatic love song to God, the Magnificat.

At the end of this passage, we are told that Mary stays in the hill country for the next three months before returning home to give birth. Part of mothering God, nurturing the Divine within us, involves cultivating stillness and staying close to oneself. As much as Incubation involves the search for meaning, it is also a gestation period. It is here that the image of the chrysalis—the seed encased, and something new, often radically different about to emerge—so clearly captures the Incubation stage. A burst of activity may immediately follow the Call, but thereafter, it may be necessary to remain quiet for a time. Although the seeds of the unexpected have been planted, it is still too early to tell what kind of fruit it will bear. One can no more force the journey to its conclusion than one can reach into the earth and pull small shoots from the ground to expedite their growth. Sometimes we must wait. And this can be very challenging.

Brooke was experienced in cultivating a receptive frame of

mind and waiting for inspiration to strike, but the downward spiral of the last years left her impatient to take action. She was all the more propelled, for the bolt that pierced her heart seemed clear in its meaning, and it left an unshakable sense of direction in its wake.

> Neither the experience of the lightning bolt nor the music had any component of self-consciousness in them. They were so total. I wasn't sitting there with a reflecting mind thinking about it or wondering what it meant. I was just in the middle of it, and at that moment, it felt like the most important thing that ever happened to me. I didn't judge it from a practical, intellectual point of view. It was much more immediate than that. I knew I was in grave danger and that my children were in grave danger and that there needed to be a way out of this. I had to be highly open and prepared to see what to do.

> I asked the owner of the café about the music. He showed me a cassette box with tulips on it and at the bottom there were only the initials "R. M." I wrote that down and tucked it away in my purse and then went about the rest of the evening. I decided to keep it very private.

Brooke knew she had to find the composer of that music. In some way she could not yet explain, she knew his music would profoundly affect her future. The next morning, she began to peruse union directories for the name and address of the mystery musician. As is often true in the Incubation phase, the most direct and logical approaches prove unsuccessful.

> I figured he had to live on one of the coasts. I looked through the New York directory, Local 802, but didn't find his name. I looked through some smaller ones, and ones for Los Angeles, but couldn't find a thing. After searching for a while, I realized that I wasn't going to find him in any linear fashion.

I knew that if I didn't do something, go out and make something happen . . . an opportunity would pass me by. I didn't want to be depressed and stuck forever, but I just didn't know what to do.

Brooke was stymied. The impulse to act was strong, but the form and the direction were a puzzle. Her initial efforts had ground to a halt and she was forced to stop, surrender normal problem solving, and wait until some deeper insight emerged. Fortunately, it didn't take long.

I began to reflect on some of the most important things I'd learned about music and performing. Practice was one. There was simply no substitute for it. Whenever I wanted to take the next step in my technique or even in my career, I practiced. I also remembered that years before, a friend of mine, a director on Broadway, told me that in order to project your sound to the back of the concert hall, instead of playing louder, create an intense vortex of sound around you that will pull the audience in. It really works. I learned to make the sound really concentrated around me, even when I was playing soft, and I would draw people to me.

It was as if Brooke were assembling the ingredients of a mystical recipe, alchemically designed to produce an unexpected gem. She couldn't rationally explain her paradoxical logic, but within her, she felt certain that the road to this musician began with solitude and practice. Somehow, its intensity would bring about the desired result. She didn't know how, or when for that matter, but she began.

I got up at five in the morning, so I'd get two hours before the children would get up, and then I'd practice while they were in school. I was practicing four to six hours a day. It was a very private experience. I wanted to create a certain quality of sound, and also overcome the last of the technical difficulties that were involved in flute playing.

It was like a fork in the road, and at each turn, you just had to take one next step. There was a lot of blind faith and not knowing if it was leading anywhere at all. But it felt like the only thing to do. In every instance where something had gone terribly wrong in my life, music was the lifeline. That was what I had to constantly remind myself. It was the only way that I ever saved myself.

Brooke threw herself into practice. There was little time left over for socializing, and since the event at the café, there was no one in particular whose company she really desired. Her time belonged to her two children and to the silver flute that waited in the basement for her each morning.

William Bridges, author of *Transitions,* tells us that the Incubation period is not only a period of social separation, but spatial as well.

More than simply out of contact with [one's] peers and his elders, [one] is absolutely and radically alone . . . out of relation with all others. In space, too, he is beyond the edge of his old world. There is no map on which one could point and say, "There he is." There is no *there,* there, since he inhabits for this time a non-place.[18]

To the casual observer, her family's basement looked quintessentially ordinary. The closets had become overstuffed with photo albums, the children's early drawings, and science fair projects. The corners were stacked with boxes of old clothes, and a small gym set stole the room's center, the gleaming chrome betraying its lack of use after an initial spurt of enthusiasm. Although heated and carpeted, the floor felt unforgiving after practicing for many hours, and as summer moved into fall, it took longer to play the cold out of her fingers.

As uninspired as it may have appeared, the basement had become her sanctuary, protected from the strain of the marriage and the responsibilities of parenting. It was like an autohypnotic technique; with each step Brooke descended in the morning, she felt more and more relaxed. By the time she reached for her flute, she felt alive again, and excited to play. After ten months, practice had become an end in itself. Brooke had accomplished the technical goals she had set for herself. For the first time in years, she agreed to perform. Just before that evening, however, a synchronous series of events unfolded.

> My husband was in the advertising business. He relied upon me to be in charge of musical decisions for commercials and the like. He met a woman at a seminar he was attending, and after they had talked for awhile, she gave him a tape to listen to, and he brought it back for me to hear. I didn't recognize the cover, or the style of music, and all it had was a business name, Illumina Music Works. It was a demo tape from this company. My husband asked me to go and meet the musician, who, coincidentally, lived just on the other side of town.

> A few mornings later, I found his office in a group of condominiums. The door was open, and I went in. I heard some music and followed it down this narrow staircase into the basement, to a small studio. The musician had headphones on, and his back to the door, so he didn't know I was there, and I stopped just to take in the scene. I think it struck me before I realized what was happening. The walls were covered with tape racks up to the ceiling, and between them, cases of cassettes, hundreds of them, with the cover that I had seen in the café almost a year before. I'm not sure the whole thing had time to reach my brain, but I suddenly burst into tears. I had found him!

The sights and sounds that Brooke registered neatly formed the threads that wove together a year's worth of practice and trust. The Incubation period was drawing to a close. For Brooke, the journey of the last ten months was beginning to make sense. The unsuspecting musician, however, was haplessly confused.

> He must have sensed something. He turned around and took off his headphones and there I was, sitting on the stairs, sobbing! Later he told me, he was actually kind of frightened. He thought I was insane. Some crazy, distraught housewife, which at that point, wasn't far from the truth! He was polite, but only because I was a prospective client. I gave him a flyer for my upcoming concert, but he actually doubted that I really did play the flute.

Ricardo was busy. There were a number of commissioned pieces he needed to finish, as well as a few film scores. He had taught himself to work through the night to make his deadlines, but at this point, it seemed he needed every hour of daylight as well. By the evening of the performance, he had completely forgotten. It was only because a friend had called to remind him that he reluctantly attended the performance. As it was, he arrived with only fifteen minutes to go.

It had been a great evening, and Brooke was thrilled to be performing again. It seemed a lifetime since she'd been on stage, yet it felt like she was returning home. With the exception of the hours practicing, there was no other place or activity she knew so completely. Brooke chose the Poulenc for her finale. Of all the pieces in her considerable repertoire, the demanding "Sonata for Flute and Piano" would both test her technical proficiency and display the rapture she felt in performing again. Long before it became a favorite of soloists on the concert circuit, she had chosen the Poulenc as her signature piece, and as the evening drew to a close, she poured herself into its haunting melodies and breathtaking runs. It was about this time that Ricardo arrived and quietly took a seat in the back. As he recalled:

> I was expecting a housewife who played part-time. Somebody wealthy perhaps, with time on her hands; an intermediate student of the flute . . . making the notes but without any particular tone or spark. You know, like sitting through a child's recital. You want them to do well, but they are just barely getting through it. I also expected the music to be old and tired. I was a composition major in music school, but most of the classical literature didn't really speak to me anymore.

> The whole thing really blew my mind! The music was very contemporary and complex. She played it up tempo, and it was only then that I realized what incredible facility she had. She really *was* a professional. I think she mentioned she had been to Juilliard. I had too. I'd gone in many times, sat in on some lectures, but I didn't really think she graduated from there!

A reception followed. Flushed and exhilarated, Brooke received congratulations from family, friends, and patrons of the arts throughout the county. It had been a small venue, but Brooke felt as fulfilled as she had in many of the country's premier concert halls. Ricardo waited his turn and then approached.

> At the time, I was composing very slow compositions, with long melodies. It would not be a technical challenge for her at all. I was doubtful that she really did want to work with me.

As Brooke remembered:

> I had played my heart out. It was such a great feeling to be back. He looked a little surprised and unsure when he came

to say hello. He asked me: "Are you sure it's *my* music you want to play?" I said yes. So he began writing for me. A few days later we actually played a little concert together and shortly thereafter, we began to record the flute part over the gray line I had seen in the vision. That became the opening cut of our first CD.

A circle was complete. Brooke emerged from Incubation. She began to perform and produce music as a full-time professional again. This time, however, she leaped from the formal confines of classical music to the as-yet-undefined arena of new age and world music. It was a big jump for someone formally trained, but their collaboration seemed the fulfillment of her vision. Her prayer had been answered. The music hadn't died. In fact, like the phoenix, it had arisen again in magnificent form. Still, the ferocity of pain and grief in ending her marriage would stun her upon returning from a day's work at the studio. After fifteen years, the end was a certainty, but the requisite steps were not. The distance between the exaltation of composing and the death of her marriage was almost too much to bear, and Brooke knew that it was only the music that enabled her to withstand the stress.

> It was very difficult. Again, it was step by step, a tremendous leap of faith. There was taking care of the children and trying to shield them as much as I could. Then there was the fifteen years of sitting on my fury, and, as the marriage dissolved, I was, for the first time, telling him what I really thought. And I was furious! I would pursue him around the house, trying to explain what was crumbling around us, and then he'd get furious.
>
> There was also an enormous force of doubt that exemplified ending a long marriage. But I didn't feel there was any other choice. I could sense that the doubt was there, hanging like a huge monstrous, shadowy ghost, but it didn't feel like *mine*.

In fact, I don't think there was a moment when *I* felt doubt. There were just times when I didn't know what to do next, or how to do it. When that would happen, I would just tell myself, "You just have to concentrate on the music." When things got really complicated, I'd focus on that.

The conflict rose to a frightening pitch. Neither one could imagine sustaining the enmity much longer. Indeed, it seemed the very walls of the stone house were about to explode. One day, after driving the children to school, Brooke stopped along a country road, unwilling to, once again, drive home. She finally surrendered to a certainty she had kept at bay for over a year, and once released, it came with a torrent of tears. She realized a decision had already been made. She could not wait. It would have to be her to leave.

I saw that my husband's economic future was in grave doubt. He seemed less and less able to function, and he was now working for his parents in a very volatile environment. I knew that I'd have to support the kids, and I knew that the only way was through my music.

I also saw that if we continued, the children would be more hurt, and that it could be possible that my leaving might be a liberation for them too, if not immediately, eventually. I began to tell them the truth of my feelings and my plans, and to my surprise, they began to encourage me.

Purged, Brooke allowed her tears to dissolve into the silence of the suburban woods. Brooke felt comforted, and a calm enveloped her. Just then she noticed a deer standing off to her right, watching, seemingly connected, as if sharing her thoughts. Perhaps it was just convenient, but she distinctly felt this regal creature assuring her.

If it was just once, I don't think I would've given it much credence. But it continued to happen. Often I'd be driving, thinking of something, and come to a stop sign, and a deer would be standing there. They never ran away, even when I got out of the car. It seemed to be a confirmation of some sort.

The language of an artist's life is filled with nuance and suggestion. A child's voice can inspire an aria, an errant phrase, a story. Brooke had learned from her experience in the café. It was possible that the most important events of our lives are little understood at first. Even more than the particular message, the greater legacy of the unexpected is a respect for the unknown and its life-changing potential.

A few weeks later, I was driving on a road in town. No trees, not much land to speak of. Mostly residential development. I was lost in thought again, mostly about leaving. I had driven into a cul-de-sac, and there, standing in broad daylight, was an enormous buck, with huge antlers, in the middle of the street. I stopped the car and opened the window, and we stared at each other for some time.

A few weeks later, Brooke left the marriage. It was painful, but each day seemed to confirm rather than contest her decision. Now, at least, both of them could move on. Brooke had always yearned for someone who could match her creative desire and her need to make music. She knew that if and when that would happen, the power of it would be undeniable. Eventually, the composer, whose melody had once literally taken her breath away, became her partner. Two years after the end of her marriage, Brooke and Ricardo became engaged.

Leaving was the hardest thing I've ever done. But it was the right thing for everyone. My son is in college, the youngest student to ever have won a journalism scholarship at his university. My daughter is a jewel and is living with me. We are gloriously happy, crowded together in our home and studio. We practice every day and we have become our own recording company. We've played throughout the country, and a few years back were nominated for a Grammy. Last year, we released our fifth CD, and most unexpected, at the age of forty-five, I gave birth to a beautiful baby boy.

As I continued to study accounts of the unexpected I was surprised to discover that although the wildly fantastic stories were riveting, I was more drawn to tales in which, not one, but a series of events occurred. Together, they seemed to point in a direction never considered, along a path not before seen. The chronicles of Christopher and Tara fit this category, as does Brooke. Catherine's tale is remarkable because the cumulative impact of a number of experiences initiated such a dramatic life change, and because the unexpected had to penetrate the nearly inviolable fortress of military convention.

Catherine

MILITARY INTELLIGENCE

"And in the Spirit, he carried me away
to a great, high mountain, and showed me the holy city . . .
its radiance like a most rare jewel, like a jasper, clear as crystal."
—REVELATION 21.10,11

Military Intelligence. Interpreter. Document translation and tape transcription. Top Secret Clearance. I speak French, German, and Czech. I was in for ten and a half years, most of that time stationed in small intelligence sites dotted throughout Germany.

Catherine is a round-faced, forty-year-old woman, nearly five feet ten inches and of stocky build. Her shoulders and arms are muscular. They suggest someone capable of hard work; a willingness to assume responsibility; someone who can perform under pressure. Catherine is a cheery sort, amiable with a winning smile and quick to laugh about herself. Her eyes hold mine with an incisiveness, and she speaks with precision and clarity. But there is also a wistful quality to her. Beneath her eloquence and ease of demeanor, there is a yearning when she speaks of the spiritual side of her life.

Catherine's story summarizes the classic elements of the Incubation phase: the feeling of disorientation after the entrance of the unexpected; the difficulty communicating the substance of the adventure; and finally, entering into a world of meaning imbued with its own symbols, its own unique language, and its own cryptic directionals.

Catherine's family moved frequently during her childhood. Her father, a correctional officer, would find better employment in another part of the state, and the family would follow. Already an introspective child, each relocation seemed to send her further inside. The final move, during adolescence, was to Wheeler Ridge, a small town on the edge of the Mojave Desert.

> From the day we arrived, I began to plan my escape. I knew people who had graduated high school and joined the army. You got a stipend, a college education, and if you made the right choices, you got to travel.

Catherine enlisted in the military, an informed choice, freely made, with an eye toward professional training and the opportunity to leave home. Catherine loved to read, and she discovered a fine technical aptitude and a particular affinity for Romance and Slovak languages. Tours of duty would send her to Europe and during time off, she loved to explore out-of-the-way hamlets and visit their churches. There, in quiet moments, she was reminded of her childhood ruminations, the fascination she had with things holy. In addition, she would notice that each church seemed to have its own distinct energy, and in some unexplainable way, she was able to sense its character and know the details of its past.

> My religious upbringing was slipshod. My parents never made much of an effort. I would visit the churches that had chanting and organ music. I had always been fascinated with nuns and monks. My family was not Catholic, and I think my mother just thought it was a childhood fixation. In school, when kids would draw tanks and planes, I would be drawing hooded figures with robes and bare feet. I think if I were born in an earlier generation, I would have become a priest or a nun. The old churches in Europe were like museums to me, and it felt like I could pick up feelings about their history, and the people who had prayed there.

> I would often go to this cathedral in Augsburg, in Bavaria, Germany, about thirty or forty miles directly west of Munich. The church had been built on a site of a Roman temple, over two thousand years old. Augsburg was named after the Roman general, Augusta. The city was called Augusta's Treasure City because it sat on the Lech River, and Augusta controlled all the commerce there. Before that it had been an ancient Celtic site, so we are talking about three millennia. I was captivated by the energy of this church—it had such a vibrancy to it. I went all the time, but when I was there, I would be puzzled. Although I was most always alone, it would feel to me that hordes of people were incessantly trooping through the sanctuary—like Grand Central Station. It would feel crowded and dusty, and noisy even though it was actually very quiet inside. Later, after doing some research, I discovered that the church actually straddles

the old Roman Highway. It was built directly on top of the road. That was just one experience of many. I didn't yet recognize how psychic I really was. I didn't know about these things yet.

After four years, Catherine had completed her first tour of duty and, while awaiting her next assignment, she was transferred to the military language school in Monterey, California. Catherine was happy with her career, but her love life was in shambles.

I had been recently divorced. I was in a new relationship, and he was just divorced. In reality, we shouldn't have been together. Each of us was so consumed and hurting. He was in the service too, and we were trying to get our careers lined up 'cause I was on one coast, and he was in Fort Meade, on the other. I had this friend, he was kind of a fundamentalist, and he saw that I was having a real hard time. He had just returned from an evangelical rally with Jimmy Swaggart. That was before his fall from grace. He suggested that I take some time out and go ask God for help. Well, I wasn't at all into that born-again stuff, but asking for help struck me as a novel idea. It had never occurred to me, and maybe because he was so enthusiastic, I decided to do it. I think he'd be very surprised to have known what happened next!

The afternoon was hot and windless. Catherine thanked her friend for the suggestion, but didn't betray what she had planned to do. It was a Sunday. The base was quiet as many of the personnel had left with their families, so she retired to her room, closed the door and laid down on her bunk. About to pray, Catherine was surprised to notice that although she had been fascinated with religious life since her childhood, she didn't really know if she believed in God.

I basically said, "OK God, I'm not sure you're really there, but I need to know what's going on." Suddenly, this feeling

came over me. It was like a light flooding me, flooding my
entire being. It felt like every neuron was firing at once and
I felt myself being lifted out of my body, into the air, and
through the ceiling. I had no idea about out-of-body experiences, so I was pretty frightened at first. I looked back,
and I could see through the roof, at my body lying there. I
thought, *Well, this must mean I'm dead or dying,* and instantly
I had this thought, as if it was a voice answering through
me: "No, you're not dying. Your body will be cared for. It
will still breathe and your blood will circulate. You'll be
watched over. You'll be fine." The feeling of it was warm,
caring, and it seemed like it was making an effort to be
nonthreatening. But it definitely wasn't my kind of thinking,
so it was pretty weird. Nothing like this had ever happened
to me before!

Catherine was alarmed, but she perceived that whatever was
speaking through her was attempting to be gentle, and this out-
weighed her fear. Even more curious, she somehow understood
that she could allow the adventure to unfold on its own, or
stop anytime she wished.

At each point, it was my decision to proceed or not, and I
had the distinct impression that at any time I could say, "This
is *too* weird . . ." and stop. The next instant, I had landed in
this meadow. The grass was fairly long, and the earth sloped
uphill. There were yellow flowers everywhere. I could feel
the grass on my feet, and I could feel wind, and as I looked
down, I realized that I was nude! Somehow, it didn't matter.
I started walking up a hill and I saw a figure at the top of
the hill with a white robe on and long red hair and I thought,
I'm not alone. I started walking toward him, and he held out
his arm and he had another robe on it. He said, "This is for
you," and I said, "OK." I remember thinking about it for a
second, trying to get a sense of whether it was safe, but I
continued to get these warm, supportive feelings from the
scene and now this man. I decided it would be OK and the

next moment, I was wearing the robe, and lo and behold, it fit perfectly! It was intensely white; white beyond white.

The experience continued to evolve, each step a bit more fantastic and abstruse. It was light years beyond anything Catherine had ever imagined possible, but as the adventure progressed, she found her bearing and poise. At each juncture, she cultivated both courage and an openness to whatever would transpire.

> By this time, I was awestruck. I had left fear behind. It seemed that I somehow kept getting reassurance from this being. By this time, I was really curious about him. I thought it might be Jesus, but I couldn't see his face. I asked, "Do you have a face?" and the reply was, "Well, yes I have one, but you're not capable of perceiving it," to which I responded, "OK. That's interesting." And again, he waited, and I was given a little time to decide if I wanted to continue. I decided, "Yeah, I can do this," and he turned and walked up over the crest of the hill.

Catherine hesitated for a moment, as if to let me catch up. She knew the tale sounded extraordinary, and perhaps she wanted to sense if I believed her. Tears began to fill her eyes. It was like a sacred amulet or rosary. When Catherine touched this part of the story, she felt the most moved.

> I followed him, always at a distance. When we got over the hill, I could see, fanning out to the horizon, this immensely beautiful city. It stretched as far as the eye could see. There weren't many buildings, so it wasn't your normal idea of a city, but I got this sense there were many, many beings there, engaged in purposeful activity. I could see lights moving; they seemed like little pockets of energy coalescing. Somehow, I knew that what was going on there was very

important. The last thing I remember, the being looked over his shoulder at me, and kept walking. Suddenly, I came to.

It was fundamentally different than waking from sleep. Usually when you wake from sleep, your startled reflex comes up, or you feel groggy coming out. With this, there was no transition. One moment I was in the scene, the next I was in bed and was very clearheaded.

Catherine "awoke" two and a half hours after she originally lay on the bed. When she first began praying, she felt tired, angry, and fearful. She felt very different now.

Very peaceful; confused a bit, but very peaceful. I had the feeling that I had been given a great gift, that I had been shown a lot of things that I would always have inside, but that I couldn't recall just yet. I'm sure I went into the city. We were close to it when I came out of the scene. There was a feeling that although the details weren't clear, when I needed to know what I had been shown, it would be there. I felt awe and gratitude.

In its own language, the vision was a response to her prayers. Instead of offering a direct reply to her relationship dilemma, however, the scene provided a larger frame with which to view her life, and a foreshadow of the journey to come. It didn't concern money, career, or romance. It portrayed a woman in the vestments of a spiritual seeker, and showed her she wasn't alone.

Common to many who have experienced the unexpected, Catherine felt clarity and confusion; she was elated and somewhat disoriented. She believed that what transpired was more than a dream or hallucination. Subsequent forays into consciousness-altering only reinforced that.

I've since had powerful dreams, done intense breath work, very intense meditation practice. Once someone gave me a hallucinogen without my knowledge or consent, something I wouldn't recommend, but the vision was unlike any of these. It was vastly different than anything else.

Catherine attempted a return to normal life, but it no longer seemed to fit. She was powerfully stirred, "quickened"[19] as was said during the time when many of the churches Catherine visited were built. In addition, the vision had profoundly altered her sense of scale. The immense and powerful network of military intelligence suddenly seemed diminished by the magnificence of the city on the hill and the resplendence of the being who guided her. A transformation had begun, but she had little idea what to do from here. She decided to talk to others who might have had similar experiences, in hopes that she might discover a context with which to understand what it all meant.

> For a little while, I was afraid I had a multiple-personality disorder, or was schizophrenic but that didn't seem to fit. I seem to be sane in every other part of my life! But I had no frame of reference for it and at the time, I couldn't place the term "vision" on it 'cause I had no understanding of that then. I also felt fundamentally changed, like my basic energy had shifted. I remember getting up after the experience and reading the Bible over dinner, and that was a bit helpful, but I still needed to talk with someone. Unfortunately, I chose the wrong person.

By this time in her life, Catherine had become habituated to hierarchical structures. Requests of all kinds were routinely taken to her superiors, and it was not uncommon for the direction of her life to be decided by a supervising officer. Her limited experience with the church reinforced this idea, so it made sense to approach a local cleric for guidance and validation.

So I talked to this Episcopal priest at this small church nearby. Boy, was that a mistake! It took me about ten minutes to tell him the story, but right from the beginning, it was clear that he didn't think it really happened. He interrupted a few times to tell me he thought it was a hallucination of some kind. Then he launched into this historical diatribe—you know, things like this have been recounted in the past, but it was different then. He was monotone, sounded like a politician trying to say words without any content. He did everything but yawn and look at his watch! He just wasn't interested. I left feeling really ripped off. I left there thinking to myself, *"God visited me, talked to me, and this man, who is supposed to be a man of God, doesn't want to deal with it!"* I wasn't sure if he really didn't believe it or whether he was jealous! I decided, *"OK, fine. I'll do it myself!"* That started me on the quest.

The consultation had only reinforced the separation so characteristic of the Incubation phase. Catherine would learn to become more discriminating in the future. For the time being, she would chart her way as best she could. Subsequent steps were yet unclear, but she knew that her vision would determine the direction of the rest of her life. At first, however, as is true for many, one becomes consumed by the desire to reexperience the event.

I craved that sense of connection, and whenever I had free time I visited churches, sacred sites, read things . . . almost anything to try to get the feeling back. It wasn't a conscious thought at first, but I couldn't ever be for very long without the feeling of spiritual connection . . . with God, the divine, whatever you want to call it.

With time, Catherine became more comfortable in liminal territory. She extricated herself from relationships that created fear and sadness, and she spent more time in contemplation.

However muddled her sense of direction, Catherine began to notice changes that were occurring within her. They seemed to be fundamental, paradigmatic shifts, and they served both to validate her vision and to propel her further.

> There were four of them. First, I had a big fear of death. It started around sixteen, shortly after my family moved to the desert. I was always really afraid. I'd talk about it constantly, listening to stories about people who died, obsessing about it, feeling really threatened. It continued with me until the vision. After, I noticed I had no fear! Now, I have absolutely not a shred of fear about death. Dying may involve pain, and that's not too attractive, but when it happens, it happens.

Catherine also began reevaluating the models she had been given with which to understand her world. The vision had begun the process, but the momentum of her quest was sustained through introspection and reevaluation.

> There were three other changes. Before the vision, I believed the standard Christian view—that you have this life, you do the best you can, you get baptized to get rid of your sins, confess the rest, and then you wait until Judgment Day. Very quickly after my experience I became dissatisfied with this paradigm. I realized that's not really the truth for me . . . maybe for someone else, but not me. Now I look at it as an allegorical expression of one aspect of the truth.

> The next change—I discovered I really had developed a sense of purpose. It wasn't so much a decision, but that I realized it had grown in me after the vision. There was a definite purpose for me in this lifetime. It wasn't necessarily, "You'll go on to be a talented musician or a great author" . . . nothing like that. It was more like, "There is a reason you are here; it's not an accident you are incarnated in this time and place with these people." I'm still finding out what that is. But for the first time, I definitely had a sense that this is where I was supposed to be.

Finally, I had a different awareness of God too. Before I thought of God as the old man with the white beard. Somebody like Thor, who would strike me down with a thunderbolt. I got a sense that God wasn't nearly as judgmental as people thought, and that forgiveness was not something that had to be earned; you didn't necessarily have to go through some ritual, some baptism, or walk on hot coals to obtain this forgiveness. I realized that there was a fundamental good there, that the universe was good, that people are good. And though they fall into error and make mistakes, or sin, or even become evil, it's their choice. But what was strongest was realizing the fundamental goodness and rightness of existence.

Acquaintances saw nothing unusual, and to her friends, she appeared more relaxed and happy, if just a bit more private. But, in the fertile depths of this reflective period, Catherine discovered one more surprise.

I discovered that I could know things about people without being told. I could hold objects in my hand and know who had held it before and what was going on with them. And this was very strong in the churches, where it seemed I could sense their history even more than before. I had the ability before, not as strong, but I was threatened by it and didn't want to experience it. Part of it was my mom, who was very psychic, and was really threatened by it. She thought it was sinful, evil, and from the devil. She didn't want to think or talk about it, but it's there.

It took awhile for Catherine to overcome the mild trauma she felt during her consultation with the minister, but as if that too were part of the plan, Catherine became more self-sufficient in her quest and more committed. Once again, she was transferred back to Europe. These were the waning days of the Cold War, just before the Iron Curtain would fall, and everyone was on alert. It wasn't clear what would happen next, and Catherine and her colleagues were pressed into service, intercepting and deciphering messages of all kinds.

The global climate provided a strange contrast to Catherine's Incubation period. During the short leaves she was granted, she would once again explore old churches and spiritual sites. Her sense of the quest was strong and demanded attention. At the same time, everyone at her level of the military was under increased surveillance.

> That was the beginning of my thoughts to leave the military. I was growing too much. My interests had changed dramatically, and with top-secret clearance, you were closely monitored. I was tiring of life in the fishbowl. But it was a difficult decision. I had been to some expensive, difficult-to-get-into schools in the military, and I felt that I owed them for sending me there. Out of the ten years I was in, I spent four of them in school. I was pretty fortunate. It began to occupy more of my thoughts though, and I started feeling like a failure of sorts. I was more and more interested in spiritual concerns, and I was growing more and more unhappy. Not the least of which was feeling in limbo.

Catherine was genuinely torn. There were still two years remaining on her tour, so although she worked diligently to achieve clarity, she knew that nothing material would happen for a while. She could feel the direction of her heart, but she could not imagine leaving the service. Catherine thought perhaps the fervor of her quest would mellow, and she could accommodate it to the demands of her job. She wondered about transferring to another part of the military, but of all the various assignments an officer could have, she had to acknowledge that this was clearly one of the most exciting.

The decision would not be rationally made. Catherine was becoming more comfortable in the subterranean realms of the spirit, and time and again, she would return to the crest of the hill and the lights of the city for inspiration and guidance. The unexpected branded her with a dramatic sense of widened possibility, and she somehow knew that, if she remained faithful to it, she would find her way.

> Everyone has the potential, I think, but some are too threatened by it and won't allow it to happen. For some time, I would ask myself, "Why me? Why did this happen to me?" And the answer I would get was, "Because you asked for it." I believe that had I never asked, I would never have had the vision.

> It took some trust on my part, but gradually I came to believe that although this crotchety old minister didn't think it was real, it was. For a while, I thought, *This must sound like a bad science-fiction novel,* but it wasn't. So I became aware that there was guidance available if you ask; if you learn to listen to the still, small voice within. So that's what I was trusting, although I didn't actually know *how* I was going to make the decision about my career.

Twelve months passed and Catherine faithfully executed her patriotic responsibilities to her country. Her innate sense of fairness, coupled with years in the military, forged in her a deep moral and ethical sensibility, and she was loathe to renege on an agreement. The portent of profound political change only heightened her sense of duty. In her heart, however, she could feel the pull elsewhere. Frequent visits to sacred sites further piqued her longing for the spiritual. The direction was becoming clearer, but the location was, as yet, undefined. Just as the entire spine of Communist Europe was about to break, so too, in the intimate recesses of her psyche, the outdated structures of her personality were about to give way. Catherine would

never have imagined that they would be broken by the gossamer
weight of a dove.

> I was in my car, stopped at a light. As usual, my mind was
> running amok with my decision. Suddenly, a white dove flew
> onto my windshield and lighted there. It just stayed and
> looked right at me. Now they have doves in Germany, but
> they have very few white doves. You just don't see them
> much. I knew that because they were always a favorite bird
> of mine, and you just didn't see them there; *and* they don't
> usually hang out with you on your windshield during a
> stoplight! So there he or she was, and I just had to laugh. I
> remembered that the Bible talks about the dove descending
> to Jesus when he was baptized, and I just said, out loud,
> "OK, you have my attention. What's the message?"

In traditional Christian iconography, the dove symbolizes the
Holy Ghost. Before that, the dove was a symbol of the goddess
Sophia and came to suggest impregnation. Gnostic Christians
believed that the spirit of Sophia was incarnate in the dove that
impregnated the Virgin Mary, and it was the same dove that
impregnated Jesus' mind during his baptism by the river. In
Oriental folktales, the dove represented the souls of women
who come to rest with their ancestors after death, inside a magic
hollow mountain.[20] The endless cycle of death and rebirth was
stirring Catherine's life, and for a moment, on one afternoon
in Europe the mythic and the personal collided.[21]

Catherine's life as she knew it was drawing to a close. The
dove seemed to confirm that and, in its simple way, beckoned
her to attention. It didn't have the power of the great vision a
few years back, nor even of the psychic experiences she had
repeatedly in churches. This was more of a response to her ongoing question, expressed in a personal and highly symbolic

way. It reminded her that she was still connected to a larger current, despite the privacy of her dilemma.

> The next time it happened, it was about a year later, and I was growing more unhappy in the army. I was leaving our intelligence site early that day, driving down a dirt road near a little town called Gablingen. The site is quite isolated. There are huge antenna fields, right next to the old Messerschmidt Works, which is now in ruins. The only access road narrows and has tank traps on each side. A bit of military overkill if you ask me.

Catherine was frustrated. As she became more preoccupied with her decision, she grew more agitated, testy, and distracted. Known for her clarity of thought and ability to take declarative action, Catherine found the experience of waiting, both because of her military commitment and lack of a clear direction, to be aggravating. She was trying to be patient but being perpetually in limbo was wearing thin.

> I was driving down the road, again puzzling over my decision. I remember saying to myself, "That's enough! Let's get on with it!" and then entreating the universe saying, "Please, give me instructions!" Suddenly, this white dove flew right in front of the windshield and hovered there for a moment. I thought I would hit it and swerved. I almost drove off the road.

Catherine wrestled the car back onto the road, stopped, and turned off the motor. Very few knew the location of the intelligence station, and it wasn't likely she'd run into traffic. Her heart was still racing. The quick cycle of her breath would alternately fog and then clear the windshield. Thomas Merton has written: "God touches us with a touch that is emptiness, and empties us." Although it wasn't a momentous event, just mildly startling, Catherine noticed something inside her had changed. Her agitation had dissolved, and for the first time in months, she felt peaceful.

> I sat in the middle of the road, just sort of blinking. I knew that, once again, the presence of the dove was not an accident. I noticed that the emotional confusion was gone, and I felt very clearheaded. It seemed to have snapped me out of feeling confused and guilty, and [it freed me from] all that circular logic . . . that was so ineffective.

> It seemed to put me in this place of feeling balanced—a balanced head and heart—and I said to myself, "Yes, I really do need to leave the army now. It's just not a good thing for me to do any longer." It was almost matter-of-fact, and it had a clarity and a compassion for myself that I just couldn't muster before.

There was no need for further deliberation. Lucid and finally resolved, Catherine felt elated to be rid of the constant inner quibbling that had infected her. The feeling of relief and rightness was so strong, in fact, that Catherine was no longer bothered that the exact form of her future was unclear. The dove was a confirmation of the vision she had had years before. Its unlikely presence demonstrated to her that she was not alone, but guided. Further, she interpreted the repeated appearance of the dove to mean that she could now rest and be assured that the way would continue to unfold before her.

Upon the completion of her second tour of duty, Catherine moved back to Monterey, California. After traveling throughout the world, she was drawn to the soft and temperate sea breezes and the unlimited vistas of the central California coast. Her intimate facility with syntax and sentence structure suited her well for employment and for a while she worked as an editor of textbooks, before moving on to the more creative and gratifying children's books. In her spare time, in an attempt to return some of the bounty she reaped through her spiritual experiences, Catherine volunteered at a suicide hotline. But there was a deeper calling. Mercurial at first, it became apparent over time. In her inimitably pragmatic fashion, Catherine began interviewing priests and ministers throughout the county, to discover how each had received their Call. She compared their responses to the impulses she felt, their inner promptings to her visionary experiences, and she recognized her future.

When our interview ended, it seemed that I too, had traveled through Europe with her—through the dark and secret hallways of military intelligence, into the old stone churches that revealed ancient visitors, and even up the hill to share a glimpse of the city of light that had become her beacon. It was time for Catherine to leave. There was nothing more to add except that she had begun attending a local church that offered a shared ministry program. On Sundays, when she was asked to ascend the pulpit and lead the congregation in prayer and response, the feeling was almost as strong as the ecstasy within the vision on the hill that transformed her life.

FOUR

THE SEARCH
FOR MEANING

"Some people think that the mere act of having a supernatural, parapsychological experience is meaningful. But such an experience is just that: a parapsychological experience, and that's the end of it. Merely hearing voices does not mean that one has heard the voice of God. [Conversely] there are many people who really heard something and their very big mistake was that they didn't identify the voice."

—RABBI ADIN STEINSALTZ[1]

"Marvelous physical happenings can neither replace nor bring about understanding of the spirit, which is the essential thing."

—CARL JUNG[2]

Perhaps the greatest challenge, during the ambiguity of a passage, is to believe that we are part of a greater process, connected to a higher power or plan, or guided by some benevolent force. We can imagine that Rebecca felt forsaken as, night after night, her ship would totter on the crest of one behemoth wave after another, and then begin its mad free fall down. Jordan felt equally adrift both when he lost Lois to cancer and when his daughters responded with such vehemence. Both Brooke and Catherine spent extended periods of time in foreign territory, unable to apply linear problem-solving or take direct action. One cannot imagine a more fertile culture for the doubt and uncertainty.

If we examine this confusion more deeply, it reveals itself as a constriction of meaning. People are meaning-making creatures. We understand ourselves and the world through stories. We suffer to the degree that the understanding of our lives remains rigid and narrow.[3] Time and again, patients in psychotherapy demonstrate that the outdated stories we hold as true for ourselves can cause considerable anguish. Jung stated this even more emphatically when he wrote: "The lack of meaning in life is a soul-sickness whose full extent and full import our age has not as yet begun to comprehend."[4]

Conversely, we are able to live more effectively and enjoyably when we can see ourselves through an increasingly expanded lens. When bigger, more comprehensive frames of reference are created with which to make sense of our lives, we can move on.

The Search for Meaning is central to the experience of being fully human, for meaning is a primary vehicle by which we experience ourselves connected to something greater. (Its absence, the limitation of a broad enough context for our lives and a feeling of disconnection, is endemic to the Slumber.) We may relate to the Search for Meaning in innumerable ways, ranging from active engagement to denial, but regardless, the questions, "Why am I here?" "What is the meaning of my life?" "Why am I doing *this*?" always hover at the edges of our awareness.[5]

This is especially true in reference to the unexpected. The unexpected brings us to our edges; to a borderland between the known and unknown; to a threshold territory where familiar paths have fizzled out. Whether the terrain is ecstatic and filled with light or cloaked in darkness, we have little to guide us. The unexpected serves to highlight the exact point where our current maps end and where our sense of possibility has become delimited. It is here that we must make a powerful choice: to retreat back to more familiar confines or venture forth into the unexplored. Those who choose the latter, find themselves back in the "map room." It is time to update one's files and expand previously held ideas about the self and the world, because in the story of our lives, the context for the events we experience needs to be as inclusive as possible. For example, if Tara had never found the old man that appeared in her living room, an essential component for creating a broad enough context and for feeling connected to a greater process would have been lost. Most likely, she would have doubted the event's veracity, as well as her own sanity. Eventually, she might hope to forget the incident ever happened. For Tara, the creation of meaning contained two elements: First, she believed the event to be a calling, and she responded to its undeniable pull; second, upon meeting this man, she recognized that regardless of whether he was, in fact, her biological grandfather, he represented "belonging," proof of her connection to lineage and culture.

It stands to reason, then, that the greater the scope of our maps, the greater the possibility that we may understand the entry of the unexpected as part of the quest—not something pathological—and feel assured in the face of the unknown. But how is this accomplished? The symbol of the magnifying glass is most apposite to this stage, for it is in the face of the unexpected that, in order to successfully negotiate the passage, we must enlarge our sense of meaning and allow for the possibility that this extraordinary event is offering an extraordinary message. (To consult its derivation, in the word, "magnify," we encounter the old French *magnifier,* which suggests, "to glorify or praise"[6] or "increase in significance."[7] An even more archaic English usage signifies, "to stand in honor of."[8]) Even in the absence of a clear and definitive understanding of what has transpired, those who proceed through the Stages of Transformation, after an encounter with the unexpected, choose to believe that, rather than having been the subject of an anomalous event, they have embarked on nothing less than a journey into their truest self and toward their true calling. Here, knowledge of the great stories can be of inestimable value. Parables and tales, spiritual allegory and fables provide maps—pathways and parameters with which to evaluate the odd occurrences and sudden changes in the direction of our lives. If we can find ourselves in a portion of the great religious stories or cultural myths, we may feel reassured on the journey—solaced during our loneliness and emboldened in the face of its challenges.

The late English mythologist and writer Helen Luke[9] took this idea one step further. Having earned advanced degrees in classical literature, she foresaw the urgent need for a creation of a community in which the broadest contexts possible, as reflected in the great myths and legends, could be explored as they pertained to the psychological and spiritual journey that confronts us all. She founded the Apple Farm Community in Three Rivers, Michigan, where people lived and visited for the express purpose of studying the relationship between the timeless classics and the particular life passage they were negotiating. Through group discussion, artwork, periods of silence, and contemplation, the Farm encouraged people to develop a dialogue with the deepest parts of themselves and to find the particular stories and tales that spoke to them most directly, be they *The Divine Comedy* or *The Exodus, Perceval and the Grail King* or *The Odyssey*.

If we are surrounded by people who understand the passages that we negotiate as we grow—if we are fortunate enough to live in a subculture in which tales of the quest, of the hero's or heroine's journey, of spiritual transformation are prized and told—we may find guidance and inspiration during the times we are uncertain. When it seems we have traveled most off course, we can hear in these myths and legends that others have taken a similar voyage. Poet Philip Larkin reminds us in his poem ''Many Famous Feet Have Trod'': ''Many famous feet have trod sublunary paths, and famous hands have weighed / the strength they have against the strength they need.'' Just when we feel the most separate and forlorn, we can trust that we are part of a drama that has been enacted throughout humankind—the quest for understanding and wholeness. It doesn't necessarily ensure a safe trip, but knowing that our journey has deep historical and spiritual roots helps us realize that we are not alone. This realization can prove so powerful it can provide courage and hope, when, to paraphrase Thomas Merton, ''hope seems impossible and the heart has turned to stone.''[10]

Conversely, the absence of such a working model in our lives can have grave consequences. Without this kind of archetypal context, a pall of meaninglessness and disconnection can descend around us. The sudden turns of our lives leave us anxious, and we become fearful and avoidant of the unexpected. We are unable to see our struggles as part of a broader, deeper life journey. At worst, we may plummet into a deep existential and spiritual vacuum.

Torschlusspanik is a German word that signifies the panic that one feels when believing that a door between oneself and life's opportunities has permanently closed. It connotes the terror of disconnection that ensues when we are unable to sense continuity in the unexpected directions our lives may take. The source of such powerful anxiety is not that we have actually become lost, but that we are unable to see these events as part of a larger picture, the picture of ourselves in a passage. As Marion Woodman observes:

> The doors that were once opened through initiation rites are still crucial thresholds in the human psyche, and when those doors do not open, or when they are not recognized for what they are, life shrinks into a series of rejections. *Torschlusspanik* is now part of our culture because there are so few rites to which individuals will submit in order to transcend their own selfish drives. Without the broader perspective they see no meaning in rejection. The door thuds, leaving them bitter or resigned. If, instead, they could temper themselves to a point of total concentration, a bursting point where they could either pass over or fall back as in a rite of passage, then they could test who they are. Their passion would be spent in an all-out positive effort, instead of deteriorating into disillusionment and despair.

Edward Edinger, a Jungian analyst, describes the consequences at a societal level, when a cultural structure or predominant myth that is capable of responding to our deepest existential and spiritual questions is missing.

> History and anthropology teach us that a human society cannot long survive unless its members are psychologically contained within a central living myth. Such a myth provides the individual with a reason for being. To the ultimate questions of human existence, it provides answers that satisfy the most developed and discriminating members of society. And if the creative, intellectual minority is in harmony with the

prevailing myth, the other layers of society will follow its lead and may even be spared a direct encounter with the fateful question of the meaning of life.

It is evident to thoughtful people that Western society no longer has a viable, functioning myth. Indeed, all of the world cultures are approaching, to a greater or lesser extent, the state of mythlessness.

Western society has not been spared the "direct encounter with the fateful question of the meaning of life." And this is our crucible, for although we may lack the symbolic reference point that, in indigenous cultures, enables its members to negotiate the trials of the passage, we are not spared having to *go through* them. Instead, without an understanding of its structure, and the guidance of elders who have themselves made the journey, we nevertheless bumble through our changes.

Living in an indigenous culture might offer a great advantage. In the tribe or clan, meanings are preordained. The perennial wisdom is conveyed in creation myths and initiation rites. These stories and the rituals crafted from them form a container, a net of meaning, in which all events can be understood, no matter how bizarre.

But it is folly to attempt to clone another culture. For better or worse, ours is a more individual and more cosmopolitan path, and for each of us, the particulars of the journey will be different. When the Call comes, we must be willing to travel beyond custom, confront the unknown, and attempt to decipher its signs and symbols. That is precisely what our next two tales illustrate. Ben, an ex-alcoholic social worker, was offered the choice of life or death, and as the unexpected unfolded, he was given barely a moment to decide. Zach, now an organizational consultant, found himself in a mortal drama of escalating intensity. One moment of realization changed the course of his entire life. Although they differed in the grace and ease with which they glean meaning from the unexpected, both Ben and Zach eventually heeded its Call.

Ben

SOAPY'S CHOICE

He would have been just another entry. CDC Death Statistics, Category: "Accidents and Adverse Effects—Motor Vehicles."[11] The roads were slippery on the interstate, and traffic was moving faster than he could react to. Kansas state law prohibited the sale of alcohol on Sundays, so Ben had driven over the border into Missouri to buy some beer. The antihistamines he consumed to treat his cold only made him feel more logy, tired, and frightened to be behind the wheel.

> It had gotten to the point where my drinking was constant. It was in January. My construction company was idle and winter seemed a good time just to kick back and have fun. Pretty soon, I was partying all night, and then starting the day with beer just to avoid the hangover. The irony was that I was a drug and alcohol specialist in the army for three years! I *knew* what bad shape I was getting into, but I couldn't do anything about it. One day I overheard my little brother and his friends taking bets on how many cans of beer I'd drink by the evening. I moved closer 'cause I was kind of curious what they'd say. My brother bet on fifty-two! I said to myself, "Oh God!" I was shocked. Now, I usually finished a few six-packs even before I left the house for the bar, so later that night I ended up drinking number fifty-one. They all crowded around me for the next can and began to

exchange money. By the time I got to fifty-two, I was so nervous, I knocked it over.

The site of our interview was an old redwood deck overlooking a small pond in the Missouri bottomland. It was late May. The water was silty from the thunderstorm the night before, and the rain had dissolved the humidity of the previous afternoon. Wood drakes bounced and squawked on the water. Kites and killdeer streaked through the air, making impossibly sharp turns in the soft breeze. Leaning over the pond, redbud trees were in bloom, stunning dots of color through the vernal green of willow, walnut, hickory, and elm. This is the heartland, flush with spring, riotous activity in the broad peace of the meadow.

Ben is in his mid-forties. He is a Rosebud Sioux,[12] and his family lived mostly off the reservation, in eastern Kansas. A handsome, gentle man, a strong square jaw drops from his round face, and his black hair, flecked with gray, is cut short in front, but cascades almost to his waist in the back. Now, a social worker and single father living near the university town of Lawrence, Ben speaks slowly and softly. His laconic midwestern inflection disguises an uncompromising honesty, and a self-effacing wit.

> I had gotten to the point where my idea of time management was making sure that I had enough beer to last through the night, and especially through the weekend. I had it down to a science—figuring my pace during the day and night, and even knowing just how much to taper off by Monday so I could function if I needed to. That Friday, I had mathematically calculated what I needed for the weekend, so I didn't have to drive out of state. Everything was fine. On Sunday, when I went to the convenience store to get some ice, I accidentally dropped a large block on some cans of beer.

Four cans exploded, and I panicked! I wouldn't have enough to last the night! Suddenly, I was in my car hauling ass to Kansas City.

In an hour, Ben reached the Plaza district—impressive buildings with Moorish architecture. Well-dressed couples strolled on the sidewalks, in and out of cafés. He felt strangely separate from them, as if he were watching a movie. He drove past the university, into Westport, a newly revitalized district in the heart of the city. Students in jeans and winter coats walked arm in arm or huddled in coffeehouses for animated discussion. Ben noticed their ease and intimacy with one another. For a few moments, he allowed himself to feel a faint longing. As if startling awake, though, he quickly returned to the purpose of his mission. Ben didn't really want to sightsee, and it was just fine with him not to run into friends or relatives, many of whom lived in town.

> Then I found myself in the slummy parts of town, where the winos hang out. I remember looking at them and thinking, *they're no different than me, except that I got a car and go to work, and they panhandle.* I thought at one point, *I'll just park my car and live here.* I felt akin to them.

It was as if Ben was registering impressions from behind a one-way mirror, his subjects unaware of the cumulative impact they were having on his afternoon sortie. At each stoplight, Ben could sense a battle developing inside: one part frightened that his supply would run dry, while the other desperately wanted to break through and stop the cycle of dependence. Ben tried to remember the past, albeit temporary, successes he had enjoyed in quitting alcohol. Like Soapy in O. Henry's famous "The Cop and the Anthem," what Ben realized surprised him.

How had I ever stopped before? I got arrested! Those were the only extended periods of time I'd been sober in years. And I realized, I'm in prime shape to get arrested. I'm just down here driving around. I've been drunk for days now and I'm thinking, *It's cold and it's gonna be a long winter if I'm this bad off.* So I pull up to a green light and wait. I wait until it turns red and then I drive through it. But there is no one watching. So I do it again at the next light. Again, no police there. And I do it again, and then again. I'm drivin' around thirty or forty minutes doing this, thinking, *Where's a cop when you really need one?* Finally, I had to give up!

Ben's plan failed. He found a small liquor store, procured the remainder of its beer, and set off on the highway for home.

The traffic was really zipping along. One guy passed me at a pretty good clip, so I got in behind him. I decided, "He's gonna be my path all the way through and I'd make it home." So I'm behind him, cruising along real well when the Dristan and Contact I've been taking for my perpetually runny nose kicks in.

I start falling back in traffic and start to get worried that I'm gonna fall asleep before too long. I need to do something, so I think if I could just get to the next rest area, I'll be able to kick back and drink a few beers and I'd be OK. So I'm thinking about this, not really looking at the road, when I notice that traffic has slowed almost to a stop. The guy I was following has his brakes on. I looked ahead and saw a highway patrol with his lights on. It was a speed trap, and everyone was throwing out the anchor to slow down. I hit my brakes as hard as I could, 'cause I was about ready to go into the guy's trunk, and the car veered to the right. Just swerved right onto the shoulder. I did my own mechanicking [sic] in those days, and I'd done the brakes several months before. It was about a three six-pack job. That explains why it swerved. I looked ahead and then I could see the police clearly. And I could see that between me and them was a ravine.

Ben estimates his car was traveling about fifty miles per hour, but a plan was forming within him just as fast. He hadn't thought about it before, but it would solve his problem with alcohol. In fact, it would ensure that he would never have to deal with it again. Ben felt a mad surge of energy, and then accelerated toward the yawning cavity.

> It was an open ravine, with concrete retaining walls. I was thinking that this was the opportunity to end it. This was one way it was OK to die. So I went barreling down toward the ravine, and everything started to slow down. I was thinking about killing myself, but at the same time, memories of my life began to appear in my mind.

Time seemed to bend and then curl around itself. In his headlong suicide drive of the present, he met himself as he was in the past. Scenes unfolded and seemed to play themselves out irrespective of how long he had before impact. It was as if, deep within the unconscious, a part of his psyche had an urgent message to send and it would even violate the laws of physics to do so.

> This memory came up and played itself out, the whole memory. When I was in the army, we had sponsored some orphans to come out on Thanksgiving, for dinner and presents and play. I was nineteen and immature, and I was really hoping for a sixteen- or seventeen-year-old orphan girl to sponsor, but what I got was a twelve-year-old boy. I was disappointed at first. We couldn't even understand one another, because he only spoke Spanish. But I remember having so much fun with this kid! The army lays out good stuff on Thanksgiving, and I was just filling his pockets with nuts and raisins and fruits that he liked. As I remembered

this, I had an awareness that there was this wonderful person inside me and that I had to save him.

But suddenly I'm barreling toward this concrete retaining wall again. Things are back in complete fast motion, regular time, and it's really close and I really had no option other than to turn the wheel as hard as I could. It had been raining and the shoulder was soft, and the car just dug in; the front of it just dug in and started flipping. I remember being pretty much conscious the first number of flips, and then I saw that I was flipping into an oncoming lane and cars were coming at me. I threw myself down across the seat. Then there was nothing.

Ben had seen a lot during his life. He spent time in the army. He had been married and divorced. He had been present at the birth of his cherished daughter, and he had seen friends and family die. Although he had heard stories of elders on the reservation and their encounters with spirits and demons, he had never heard anyone describe anything that resembled the extremes he was about to experience.

My next awareness was hearing the crackling sounds of police radios. I'm hearing them say: "There's no hurry. There's nobody alive in there." I was terrified. I'm yelling, "*I'm* alive in here!" I remember trying to yell, thinking I was yelling, but no one could hear me. And then suddenly, I was back in the middle of the car wreck again—in the middle of the flip, right before I could see oncoming traffic—and I dove onto the seat. The whole thing replayed itself! Except for one difference.

This time, I was sitting up on the dashboard of my car, like I was a little gnome, looking at myself. The whole scene was bathed in light, really bright. At first I thought it was the sun, but the sun was nearly down and wasn't coming in any of the windows. And there was this eeriness, like all the sound of the world was there, or all the vibrations that are available were there, and they were all there at once, but it made everything *silent*. And I could see myself lying down across the seat, down where I had thrown myself. Then I heard a voice and it said: "You can quit drinking or you can die." It sounded so loud, like it was coming from everywhere. I thought everyone in the world must have heard it. Except that it was also *so incredibly quiet* that I knew it had to be coming from the very center of me. So I had these two polar opposites happening in me at the same time.

Dark became light. Fast became slow. Silence emerged from the sound of everything. Ben had entered a private world, a sacred world whose only focus was the understanding of a simple truth. After decades of addiction, and the disintegration of a kind and gentle man, it seemed that nothing less than a collision between the forces of life and death could save him.

Ben understood. He had been given an imperative to change. But that mandate was preceded by a witnessing period, a time for him to dis-identify calmly from the addiction he nurtured, to watch and then assess what was about to transpire.

It wasn't scary. It was pleasant in a way. It had this showering-down type of feeling. Everything stopped. The car seemed to have stopped in midflight, and I was hanging upside down. I remember feeling as though I wasn't very attached to myself. I was really pretty neutral about whether this body lived or died. I felt pretty matter-of-fact about it, like being offered a Pepsi or a Coke. You know, which one of these two do you want: You can quit drinking or you can die.

An instant later, I was back in my body, and I was able to sit up, get back behind the wheel, and hold onto it really tight to brace myself. I had done construction work for many years, so I was pretty strong. As soon as I was in that position, the whole thing started to go into fast motion again. The first thing that happened was that the car hit the ground, and the roof was crushed into the seat just where I had been lying down before. If I had still been lying down, I would've been flattened. I would've died.

Radical events jettison people beyond conventional reality, and into the liminal phase. Time and space become profoundly altered. Simple words and phrases acquire the deepest possible significance. Appearance, status, class, and even one's very name becomes immaterial. In essence, the separation and the Incubation stage that follows divest us from all that interferes with a truer apprehension of the world—and who we essentially are. The liminal phase can be dehumanizing but there is at least as much gained as lost. Dead to one's ordinary world, one becomes alive to the animated world of the spirit. One walks shoulder to shoulder with powers of life and death, lives in the world replete with visions and esoteric symbolism. In tribal cultures, initiates perform rituals to deepen one's connection with nature, and they become bonded with others of similar experience. As the late anthropologist Victor Turner wrote of initiates about to embark on their passage into the liminal:

> They are stripped of names and clothing, smeared with the common earth rendering them indistinguishable from animals. They are . . . at once dying from or dead to their former status and life, and being born and growing into new ones.[13]

Liminal space offers the opportunity to step outside ourselves. We gain some distance, *dis-identify* from habitual notions of who we are and how the world is supposed to work, and are able to evaluate our lives from a far broader perspective.

The grail uncovered here will be of inestimable value upon one's return to the world.

The choice was clear. Ben could surrender or cling to his addiction and the enfeebled personality on which it fed. As in the eye of a hurricane, there was no sense of pressure, only the feeling of infinite space; only a question asked and the provision of a few moments with which to consider. Ben chose life, and in some unexplainable way, he had been given another chance. When the car stopped tumbling, he was no longer imprisoned on the front seat, listening to the police pronounce his death. Instead, he broke the glass of the window, incurring his only injury, and crawled out.

> I squeezed through the window, cut my hand a bit, and then fell flat into a huge mud puddle, headfirst. When I stood up, I was quite a sight—brown and dripping wet from head to toe. I could hear these guys standing around with their backs to me, saying that they thought the car flipped about eight times. An ambulance driver saw me first, and his jaw dropped. Then the highway patrolman turned and said, "What the . . . ?" He told his buddy to turn around and look, and they were all looking like they were seeing a ghost.
>
> So I start slopping my way through the mud to get to them, and one officer, he was so compassionate, yelled, "Don't move! Don't move! Be careful!" And I kept saying, "I'm all right. I'm all right." Then I got within smelling distance, and his demeanor suddenly changed. He shouted: "You're under arrest!"

Ben paused. I was startled to find we were still sitting on the deck—that it was late spring, not winter, and that I was listening to a composed and intelligent man cogently describe a story and not gazing upon someone covered with mud. We both stole a moment to ourselves. Ben looked away, half-chuckling to himself about how wild the tale sounded. For some reason I couldn't identify, this seemed to be an interlude, and not the end of the story. Ben seemed to be deciding how to continue, and I had a question concerning meaning: "How do you understand what happened there?" Ben offered a simple answer, but one with profound implications:

> It was immediately clear to me when it happened. I believed that, somehow, I was taken back in time, to make a decision. I got a chance to feel some compassion for myself and was shown how close I was to dying, one way or another. I decided right there to quit drinking. When I was asked the question, I chose life. Somehow, in some way I don't know, it changed the sequence of events in the future, and I got a second chance.

It could be that the mind is capable of a rapid-fire presentation of possible outcomes during moments of crisis. These would have to be registered with lightning speed, reflected on almost instantaneously, and acted upon in a moment. It is possible, since we know that, in the REM cycle of sleep, the mind is able to present intricate plotlines, multiple meanings, and a sense of a considerable expanse of time having passed, though it is possible we were only dreaming for a few seconds. The other explanation is even more intriguing. When the unexpected enters our lives, it *may* carry the power to alter the time and space as well. Is that possible? Can extreme states of body and mind be so powerful as to actually alter the inviolate dimensions of time and space? Within the hallowed confines of Princeton University, nearly twenty years of research seems to point to an answer. At the School of Engineering and Applied Sciences, a small program was founded, cryptically named

Engineering Anomalies Research.[14] The project attempted to determine if people could significantly alter the performance of computer systems through intentional thought or contemplation.[15] Conforming to the rigors of disciplined objective research, a simple but ingenious plan was developed, in which a subject, present in the laboratory or even thousands of miles away, would attempt to skew the production of a random number generator, either toward the number one or zero. Under normal conditions, a binary number generator will produce a bell-curve-shaped distribution, a roughly equal number of zeros and ones over a large number of trials. In its experiments, however, the lab discovered that, quite easily and with no previous training, an assigned subject could imagine the generator producing more of one number than the other, and as laboratory technicians observed, the bell curve would shift, favoring the number intended by the subject. In virtually every case, the shift was small, but statistically significant. The lab had proof that human consciousness could influence matter, in this case machines. But the research did not stop here. In addition, they experimented with time and discovered that people could affect the computer in the future and past as well.[16] Clearly, but in ways we can only conjecture, the human psychological processes have the capacity to render time and space as fluid and mutable.

Ben couldn't answer the question, "Who or what transported him back in time," nor could he explain how time seemed to fold back on itself in the space of a few seconds and provide him with a second chance at life. He had not reviewed the literature, nor was he familiar with the scientific precedent for his experience. But he was profoundly moved by the recognition that however the opportunity was provided, it was the self-love and compassion that had been in such short supply rather than his pessimism that emerged to guide him. When the moment of life and death came, he was presented with the very thing he despaired he had lost—his own worth—and that made all the difference. Meaning and intention became fused. Ben understood the event's meaning, and the intention to recover his life would follow.

In a simple story, Ben's adventure through time and space might have been enough to end his addiction. Stunned and grateful, he would have emerged a changed man, resolute in his abstinence and endowed with an appreciation for the preciousness of a human life. Ben's journey, however, was not that simple, nor was his dependence so easily displaced.

Nevertheless, there were some changes, however modest. Ben found himself in a familiar environment: jail. The sentence was mild, only five days, and in and of itself, not much cause for Ben's concern. He would keep to himself, and the days would pass quickly enough. This time, though, he couldn't stop thinking about his family and, especially, how crestfallen his mother would be to find that her son had once again been incarcerated. With his first phone call, Ben devised a plan. He asked a friend to call his brother to arrange for his release. He would tell the family he had an accident. No one would know differently and no one else would be hurt.

> Well, my friend asked my brother, who had been drinking. He didn't want to come to the jail with alcohol on his breath, so, without my knowledge, my friend and brother went up to my mother's house and told her. Here I was expecting

to see my brother's face, and to my astonishment, it was my mother.

It crushed me to see the level of disappointment on her face. I finally had to admit that I *was* fucking up people's lives besides my own. I had never really let that in before. You know, that had been my big lie—"I'm not really bothering anybody. I'm not hurtin' anybody but myself." Well, I realized I was hurting someone—her—and it was almost too painful to bear.

For a few moments they stood, separated by steel, but connected through the tears they shed. Ben saw the folly of his denial in the face of a suddenly old woman, modest of means, worried that life at the edge would swallow her only precious endowment—her sons.

Ben vowed then and there to stop. He returned to work and was surprised that he actually admitted to being an alcoholic. He felt great relief in giving up the denial, and it was a good first step. He knew from his experience that he was on the right track, and he consented to be the target of good-natured humor for the rest of the day. Once again, however, Ben underestimated just how serpentine addictive thinking could be. The result was telling and undeniably farcical.

I was going on a trip out of town. I had come up with this plan. I decided I wouldn't drink . . . except for hard liquor . . . and not more than one shot per hour. That way, I couldn't become legally drunk. I figured that's how long it would take for my body to process it.

We went out the first night, and I'd have a drink and look at my watch for fifty-five minutes, and then take another drink and look at my watch. So, it was working . . . kind of. Then we went to an exotic dance club and there was this absolutely gorgeous woman dancing. She was three feet away, right in front of my face dancin' naked, and I'm spending fifty-five minutes looking at my watch, and I'm thinking, *There's something not quite right here. I'm not enjoying this. I'm not enjoying life at all. Here's this beautiful naked woman three feet away, trying to get my attention . . . and I'm just looking at my watch 'cause I have a couple more minutes before my drink arrives!*

However possessed Ben was by the spirit of alcohol, the absurdity of the scene was irrefutable. He had become a caricature, a one-dimensional figure perpetually bumbling in a madcap quest for his next potion. It was not clear to Ben, nor anyone else, just how long it would continue, but friends were beginning to lose their humor, and Ben had bargained goodwill one time too many.

It was a Sunday, three weeks after the accident. I was still on the business trip. I was in Lincoln, Nebraska, also dry on Sundays. I went to visit a friend. I was hoping to sit and talk, and drink and continue my "fifty-five-minute plan." Turned out he didn't have hard stuff, just wine, and I thought that would work too. So we're at the kitchen table, and he's talking, and I'm not listening to what he's saying. I'm just looking at my watch, and I'm not noticing he's getting angry. At about fifty-four minutes, right before the next drink, he says, "And if you think you're getting my last drink of wine, you're crazy!"

Well, it unleashed in me this panic. I ran out of his house, back to the motel to get dressed to go out. I'm thinking of all these reasons I can tell the boss why I need the company pickup. I planned to drive back to Kansas City, just like three weeks before, to buy something—anything!

There was no reflection, only a frenzy of motion. The object of his desire had become an absolute obsession. If we had been quietly seated in the corner of a motel room, we would have seen the door suddenly fly open, and a blur of a figure bolt in, ripping off his T-shirt and jeans with shaking hands, muttering a plan to himself, and attempting to steady himself enough to don his socks and tie his shoes. It was then, when he least anticipated an interruption, that the unexpected occurred, one last time.

> I had just tied my shoes, and I went to get up. It was a motel with a whole mirrored wall, and, when I stood up, instead of seeing me, there was this old guy standing there. In what should've been my reflection was this old, gray-haired, gristled lookin' thing, and I just looked at it. Stunned. It wasn't someone else. It was me! My hair had become streaked with gray. My skin was this horrible ashen color. My eyes were glazed and wild.

Ben could not claim ignorance this time. The picture in the mirror horrified him. He had to admit its meaning. He could no longer run.

> That *was* me in the mirror. I hadn't really looked at myself in a while; really taken in the effect of my drinking. But there was something else just behind the image. It was death. I realized I was seeing death like a transparency, slightly offset, just behind my figure.
>
> Just then, I felt hands on my shoulders, from above and behind me, and they pushed me right back down onto the bed. I just gave up. I just went *pffffff*... like air escaping from me. I just collapsed, and as soon as I collapsed there came a thought. It seemed like my thoughts but in a voice that I had never heard before. It said, "You don't ever have to do this again."

Ben sat in silence at the end of the bed. He felt the exhaustion of weekend, the cumulative fatigue of the past few months, and the despair of years wasted with alcohol. There was no fight left. Even the attempt to rise seemed folly. He realized that he allowed his addiction, like a boa, to constrict and then suffocate whatever life was left in him. There was nothing to do but offer himself as prey and surrender.

But just as he registered his defeat, Ben recognized something about the voice that had just spoken and the force that had pulled him back onto the bed. He realized that these two events formed the continuation of the dialogue begun as he was hanging upside down in the car three weeks before.

> There was an unspoken message there. It wasn't language based, but it said to me, "Now, we made an agreement. You need to listen to it." And, you know, I *did* make an agreement in the car about not drinking, and I was being reminded of it. *That* was powerful—you know, the continuity of the message and being held responsible like that. And that was it! I've never had another drink, and I was hardly ever tempted again.

In some Native American tribes, elders use a special tone of voice when imparting important information to the children. Whether talking about animal totems or tutelary spirits, creation stories or tribal customs, the elder would gather the children and speak in a whisper. The children would have to draw close and pay attention if they wanted to learn.

The voice that spoke to Ben during the automobile accident had returned. During the months thereafter, it would offer guidance and refinement in direction. Once, when Ben awoke, frightened that he would lose his sobriety, the voice soothed him:

> I was scared, and I didn't want to get out of bed. All of a sudden I heard the voice say, "All you have to do is get back to this bed tonight without drinking and you'll be OK." I was so excited to feel that connection that I jumped out of bed and leaped into my car for work.

I spent that evening with an old drinking buddy, and I knew it was his habit to stop at the bar for his nightly round of pool. I was nervous. I didn't trust myself to go in, but I didn't want to say anything. Suddenly he said, "Would it be all right if we didn't stop and play pool tonight?" I just sputtered, "That'd be great." I went home, and I fell into bed, elated. It seemed like a monumental task to get through that day without drinking. That voice kept showing up advising me, still does sometimes. It was the same voice as the one when I was on the dashboard and the car was flipping, and it was the one in the motel. It sounded like your grandmother whispering loving things to you.

Ben felt nourished and held by this connection. His body, completely free of alcohol for the first time in years, felt lighter, and so did his demeanor. His tensile obsession had been replaced with playfulness, reason, and during times of quiet, especially on his porch overlooking the meadows and ponds, gratefulness. When we last spoke, Ben had remarried. His wife, a strong and intelligent woman with a wonderful sense of humor, whom I had briefly met during a stop in Kansas City, now completed the affectionate household of Ben and his ten-year-old daughter.

I remember having this memory. I remember watching as my parents were teaching my little brother to walk. How much glee they got out of it when he finally could put one foot in front of the other. I started thinking that whatever is up there must be feeling the same way about me.

Zach

THE VAJRA SWORD

A student approached his spiritual teacher, bowed in respect
and asked: "What is the secret of life?"
The teacher replied, "Good judgment."
The student bowed again and asked, "How do you get good
judgment?"
The teacher said, "Experience."
The student bowed one more time and queried, "And how
does one get experience?"
The teacher replied, "Bad judgment!"

The only approach was a one-lane road winding up a steep hill
above the small town, overgrown with scrub oak, cedar, maple,
and stands of eucalyptus. The harsh summer sunlight grew soft
and diffuse, and a green mist seemed to hang over this rural
suburban street. A young deer, a four-point buck, silently scaled
the embankment below, stopped in the middle of the road, and
looked at me, unconcerned. In two relaxed leaps, he climbed
the hill on my left and began to forage on some clover, occa-
sionally looking up to ascertain my progress.

My destination was the house of a forty-eight-year-old organizational consultant named Zach. The experiences he would
relate were comparatively subtle ones, excellent examples of
how the unexpected need not be wildly dramatic to be transformative. However, as his story reveals, the meaning that Zach
attributed to them initiated a profound life passage. Ultimately,
Zach provides an ongoing portrait of becoming more and more
sensitive to the meaning within the unexpected, trusting his

intuition and refining the direction of his life in unusual and iconoclastic ways. For once one understands that life by its nature is a quest for meaning and awakening, the course and the form become uniquely one's own.

Zach lives among a collection of wooden cottages that cling to a steep hillside. They have been expanded innumerable times throughout the years to accommodate friends and their children. At present, three families seem to cohabitate here in what Zach lovingly refers to as his tribe.

We have never met and have spoken only briefly by phone. His directions brought me to the house with ease, but after knocking on a number of open doors to no avail, I cautiously wandered through his home for some semblance of life. After a few minutes, deciding I had mistaken the day of the appointment, I began the circuitous return trip to the car to check my calendar. On my way out, I came to a simply apportioned living room with a soft white carpet and stopped to absorb the details: two, low-slung overstuffed chairs, a number of wood statues and masks from Africa, wandering Jew and coleus in pots hanging from the ceiling, and nestled in the bay window, on a broad, metal-and-glass coffee table, a book whose selection seemed curious—not the usual coffee table book fare. It was entitled *Ending Hunger: An Idea Whose Time Has Come.*

Engrossed in my inspection, I hadn't heard footsteps approaching, and it took a few more moments before I realized that someone was standing in the doorway. There I met Zach, awkwardly welcoming him into his own home. Psychotherapists are trained to carefully observe the patient in the first minutes of the therapeutic interview, for they provide a glimpse of one's character and are often predictive of what unfolds during the remainder of the hour. I fumbled an apology for being in his house, but despite my discomfort, I saw that he was smiling broadly, playfully enjoying my embarrassment.

This, I learned, was quintessential Zach. As we sat in his backyard to talk, he exuded both an excitement and curiosity. He struck me as someone who can be assertive and take control of a situation if need be but is also more than willing to go along for the ride, entertain the unknown, and see where the adventure might take him. I felt in him an openness, even an innocence, coupled with a keen intelligence.

This interview shared features common to most I have done. Quite often, people have one event in mind, something they are prepared to talk about. They may have even rehearsed it in their minds. Unexpectedly, something new arises on the heels of the familiar, something not recalled for many years, that adds dimension to their story and depth to the meaning of it for them. At that moment, a sense of adventure is kindled and the interview spontaneously unfolds.

Zach and I easily developed a rhythm. I would ask a question about his experiences, and he would reply in specific and then expand into whatever areas he felt were related. One memory would emerge out of the previous, revealing more root experiences and providing opportunities for him to connect them all in the broader meaning of his life. Zach began to delight in the simple sense of revelation and in appreciation for the progression of events that brought him to this point in time. To begin his story, however, it is necessary to recognize the extraordinary context in which it took place.

> I guess we need to go back to the sixties and all that turmoil. I was traveling the straight and narrow. I was in law school in 1967 at the University of Baltimore, and I was on the path of becoming a successful attorney. I had a mentor, a

friend of the family, who was a very successful lawyer and wanted me to become part of his firm. I had a fiancée who was just about to graduate college, and she wanted a ring, big time. I come from a large family, my parents, second generation Russian Jews, and they were thrilled with my career. They were busily searching the suburbs for a house I could buy upon graduation. Career, marriage, house in the suburbs. That was my path. I was thrilled, too. It seemed exactly what I wanted. I hadn't yet realized that my choices up until this point were those of my family. I had been merrily going along with other people's ideas of what I should do, and who I should be. And that included the army.

Nineteen sixty-seven marked an intensification of the conflict. Still a year before the mortal surprises of the Tet offensive, the war in Vietnam was in full swing. The United States was engaged in an massive buildup of troops and munitions, and unbeknownst to Zach, all forms of the military had been called upon to serve.

The United States was still riding the wave of, "We're gonna win this war." I didn't want to get drafted. My family did some research and advised me to enlist in the army reserves. What I didn't realize was that everyone was now being considered military. Draftees, enlisted men, reservists . . . it didn't matter. We were all military, and we were all being trained to kill.

In mythology, warriors symbolize the latent forces within the personality ready to come to the aid of consciousness; the eternal struggle of light against dark; the wresting of insight from ignorance and innocence. And although far removed from the terrifying exigencies of the external battlefield, the trumpet that heralds the imperative of our awakening evokes an inner theater, filled with its own formidable adversaries and terrors.

As Joseph Campbell observed:

If anyone—in whatever society—undertakes for himself the
perilous journey into the darkness by descending, either intentionally or unintentionally, into the crooked lanes of his
own spiritual labyrinth, he soon finds himself in a landscape
of his own symbolic figures (any one of which may swallow
him).[17]

To appreciate this perspective, however, requires that we
pan back from the drama of the moment, however compelling,
and cast a distanced eye to the unfolding events. It is difficult
to accomplish from the center of the storm, and for a young
man, born of privilege and as yet inexperienced in the world,
it was nearly impossible.

> Fort Jackson, South Carolina. Four months of basic training.
> I wasn't thinking it at the time, but I was totally at the mercy
> of what other people wanted me to do. It was really just
> another level of obeying authority. It's what I had been doing
> all along.

Before he enlisted, Zach had begun to learn the art of ju-
risprudence. He memorized the rules of evidence, and he
studied remedies, contracts, and criminal procedure with de-
termination. He threw himself into constitutional and tort law,
and was about to submit to the initial terrors of the mock trial
when he found himself, like Lewis Carroll's Alice, transported
to a bizarre and foreign place, sometimes big, sometimes small,
sometimes comical, and at other times frightening.

> And the way the army did it was that if you lived in the
> north, they would send you south to Fort Jackson, and if
> you lived in the south, they shipped you to Fort Dix. They
> took you totally out of your environment, which was smart.

The separation had begun. The bus that Zach boarded may
as well have been taking him to another land. For months to

come, nothing would be familiar. Sequestered from his family, and from the comfortable life of an upper-middle-class law student, he would have to negotiate his way alone. Unbeknownst to him, Zach began a journey much deeper than any he had conceived when he attempted to avoid the draft. It commenced with the midnight bus ride.

> The first shock was getting off the bus in the middle of the night and being marched to have my hair cut off. It wasn't long; I wasn't a hippie; I was a regular guy, with regular hair. But in the space of a minute, I was bald.

As his enforced coif seemed to suggest, he was entering this next chapter of his life, naked. The haircut and uniform rendered each soldier virtually indistinguishable from the next. It was a leveling process—the loss of individual identity and status common to the liminal phase. Speech was ritualized and for the most part tasks were performed in unison. These were the symbols of Zach's transition into this arcane world, replete with its own esoteric practices and arduous trials.

> All of my drill sergeants had just returned from Vietnam and they were battle hardened. These weren't guys who were just out on vacation. They had just seen their buddies get killed. They came back to teach us how to survive. They used real bullets over there, so we used real bullets in training. They made it clear, we were in a war. Sometimes, we were literally crawling on our stomachs at night, and they'd be firing live ammo four inches over our heads, and we could see the tracers. And you'd realize that if you raised your head just four inches, you'd be dead. We learned with live hand grenades. There were accidents all the time. Occupational hazards. If you pull the pin of a grenade and you freak out, you drop it, or bobble it, freeze up, or not throw it far enough, you're dead! History. The end. Now that was real stuff. They weren't playing. They were training us to

go into the jungles of Vietnam, and they meant it. And you know, looking back, I believe they were being completely responsible because there was a lot on the line.

Zach had a natural affinity for people, a resource that stood him in good stead in law school, and especially in boot camp. After adjusting to the physical rigors of basic training, he began to enjoy the camaraderie.

It was a mixed bag. It was dangerous, but in truth, it was also some of the funniest times I've ever had. When you bring a bunch of guys together, who really have nothing to lose—you have to remember the time, and most of these guys were draftees and quite a few of them were trying everything they could to get out, the "trouble-makers," and there were quite a few. So in Fort Jackson, I was in camp with these New York–New Jersey wiseguys . . . Italian wise guys, black wise guys, but very, very street smart, who were always looking for the angle. They really didn't really want to be there, 'cause they knew the next stop was Vietnam, and they were going for it [discharge] completely. They were hilarious. Sometimes the hardest thing was to stay in formation and not laugh.

After eight weeks of boot camp, Zach found himself in the best physical condition he'd ever known. His troop had a graduation of sorts and advanced to the next, more skill-oriented level of combat training. It was there that Zach experienced the first of two events that would change his life.

Bayonet practice. The sergeant was just doing his job, and his job that day was to teach me how to kill. I fixed the bayonet onto the rifle, I think an M-14, and here I am, with a fixed bayonet in a line of a whole bunch of guys with fixed bayonets, and the practice was learning to defend yourself —thrusting and parrying—and practicing it on a stuffed dummy.

In the rarefied spirituality of the Tibetan plateau, Buddhist iconography has been evolving for the past two thousand years. Symbols from India and Southeast Asia, the origins of the religion, intermingled with the Bon, the primitive pagan cosmology of nomadic tribes in Tibet and Mongolia. Here, the sword or scepter became a powerful symbol. More than its utility on the physical battlefield, the sword represents the slaying of delusion. The *Vajra dorje*—the scepter of diamondlike indestructibility—reflects the capacity of a clear mind to cut through the veils of illusion. Penetrating and fearless, the vajra sword destroys misconception and distortion, and it offers a glimpse of essential reality.[18]

> It took me totally by surprise. I wasn't thinking about anything in particular at the time. At the moment when my bayonet ripped through the canvas dummy, everything seemed to stand still. Everything got quiet. I didn't hear or see anything that was happening on the field. Everything froze. And I had this profound realization. I realized that I was there, on the field, but that *I* hadn't chosen it. I was in the wrong place—being trained to kill was not my path—but nobody was doing it to me. Nobody was holding a gun to my head. I *allowed* myself to be brought to this point. I was doing what others wanted me to do. Somebody thought it was a good idea to become a lawyer. I was becoming a lawyer. Somebody thought I should be married and have a house in the suburbs. I was getting married. And somebody thought it was a "good idea" to enlist, and I followed along. Now I was being trained to kill! It was such a flash of insight, like a lightning bolt. Nothing like regular thinking. At that moment, I knew, uncategorically, that when I finished basic, I would make my *own* choices.

The moment his bayonet pierced its target, Zach woke up, as if from a long dream. He was no longer the prodigal son on a short hiatus from his ascension to material success, status, and power. In a process remarkably similar to those repeated throughout time in tribal cultures, Zach was thrown into liminal territory.[19] His former identity, including his appearance, clothing, and even to some extent, his name (he was most often referred to as "private") was ripped away. He could not have become more anonymous. Zach began to realize that he was no longer the young innocent who left law school to enlist.

> It's like my eyes were opened. You know, I didn't have any other influence. My parents weren't around. My siblings or my friends weren't around. I had no other influence but myself. It was the first time I got to think about my life, out of my normal context, and what I could feel was that something was really happening—in me and out there. For the first time, I actually heard what the protests were about. I heard it in a way I had never before, and in those moments, I realized that that was me too! *I* wanted the war to end. And *I* wanted changes to happen, and I realized that I had to make changes in myself.

With these powerful insights, Zach's sense of himself rapidly shifted. As it did, he felt more connected to the tenor and spirit of life on the streets, and less to the more parochial subculture from which he came. The unexpected, and the meaning he attributed to it, had begun the process of his individuation. During the Incubation that followed, the seeds of its particular form began to germinate. Zach began to keep his own counsel and learned to value his own opinions. He felt powerfully stirred by the current social and political tumult of the times, and for the first time in his life, he knew he wanted to be a part of something.

Yet Zach was as unable to immediately translate these

embryonic discoveries into action. He had admirably survived the trials of basic training, but he was required to remain in uniform for two months more. Zach evaluated the possibilities, and then made the only reasonable decision. He'd spend time alone and reflect on the implications of his newfound awareness, and he would try to enjoy the remaining weeks.

> I knew I could only act on my realization once I got out, so there was really nothing to do but stay on the ride, do my best, and get what there was to get out of the experience. I mean, again, nobody forced me into this. So after basic, I had a lot more space to think and reflect. I was assigned clerk-typist duty, and all I did was report at 8:00 or 9:00 A.M., do my work, and then leave at 4:00. I was off for the rest of the day. It's like we graduated and were free. You couldn't go home, but life was good! You didn't have to do a lot of exercise, you did your job, and hung out with the guys. The army was a lot of hanging out. Quite frankly, it was a great male-bonding experience!

The remaining weeks flew by, and Zach had completed his training. Tie-dye subsumed his drab olive green. Chaotic dances and celebrations of love replaced battalion exercises, and protests against the war were in full swing on the streets. Popular music became a mouthpiece for a revolutionary zeal, and its lyrics took unexpected excursions into pot, politics, and consciousness. After the dual confinement of the army and law school, the possibilities appeared limitless, and everyone he met seemed flushed with the same enthusiasm and curiosity.

> Right away, I got more involved. I lived in Baltimore, so I was really close to the protests. I marched on Washington, the March. I got teargassed. I just wanted to make my presence felt. It was kinda like voting. And we did a good job. It was a pretty tumultuous period.

Zach threw his full weight behind the momentum of the times. As part of a radical personal reevaluation, he participated in marches and sit-ins, and pondered countless speeches at countless rallies. He practiced the discipline of nonviolent political protest, and studied the writings of its progenitors, Mahatma Gandhi and Martin Luther King, Jr. But as compelling as were the events of the day, Zach felt he had to understand the deeper import of the political and social upheaval that surrounded him. He desperately wanted the war to cease, and he would devote himself to that end, but even more so, he needed to discover what lay at the core of such momentous activity. Since the event with the bayonet, he knew, in a way difficult to explain, that his growth and what was happening throughout the country paralleled one another. Somehow, understanding one more deeply would lead him to the other. At the time though, Zach was puzzled how to proceed.

> The experience in boot camp opened me up a lot. For the first time, I trusted myself, I was looking for what *I* wanted to do. I was really searching. I had an apartment of my own by that time but mainly used it as a place to take dates. One afternoon, I was there alone, and I began to pray for direction, guidance, and answers. I was literally praying, which was new for me. I was saying, "Hey, I can't figure this out, I really need help."

> All of a sudden, I felt this light come around me, and *through* me. My body was filled with light and filled with this energy, like a fullness. It felt very benevolent and loving, and there was a great deal of peace and calm, and my heart opened. I didn't understand it, but it felt wonderful. I was completely altered. Everything felt different after that.

Zach wasn't sure how long he lay on the bed surrounded by the beatific light. But, of three things he was sure: One, he had never imagined such a thing could happen; two, now that it did, he could not imagine telling anyone about it; and finally, the meaning of the event was indisputable.

> I had no frame of reference for it. And I didn't talk to people about it, because I didn't know anyone who I thought would understand. I just let it be. But the meaning of it was very clear. Surrounded by the light, I felt I wasn't alone, and I knew I was being guided. Something was there with me and it felt very loving. It seemed to be saying, "Trust the spiritual path and you'll be guided." And I had no clue about that, because my religious path was not a particularly spiritual path. We were mostly political Jews in my family. It was 1968, and even though there was the free love movement, there was also a lot of upset: the war, the assassinations of Martin Luther King and Robert Kennedy, and there was a lot of talk about the death of hope. There was tremendous upheaval, but the message of the light was, "Don't invest yourself in that. Don't get caught up in that," more than I already was. I needed to find my spiritual path, and that's where I needed to put my energy. And from that moment on, that's what I did.

Zach proceeded with confidence. He knew that the light was the experience he'd been waiting for. It had brought him to the portal of a body of wisdom that would finally explain his life and times at the greatest depth possible. Absorbing the perennial philosophies became his primary interest and his quest.

> There is a saying, "When the student is ready, the teacher will appear." Well I was ready. I was ripe. And suddenly there were some amazing opportunities that showed up in my life. I came out of the light experience, and just a few days later, without looking for it, ran across a brochure of a spiritual university in Baltimore. Some of the most adept spiritual teachers from many traditions, East and West, were

teaching there. Immediately, I knew I needed to be there. I left law school and went to metaphysical school! I used the next three years to go to that school. It was the one I really wanted, and it was the information I needed.

Zach immersed himself in his studies, reading everything from the Desert Fathers to the Gnostic Gospels, the *Bhagavad Gita* to the *Tibetan Book of the Dead.* As the university endeavored to journey into the mystical foundations of the great religions, each student also received instruction in meditation and prayer. Zach discovered questions he had never even entertained, and found a spiritual underpinning to the world that seemed to explain its darkest and brightest moments. Law school had been designed for success in work, but these studies spoke to his soul. Zach was finally following his own intuition, his own heart, and it was thrilling.

The discovery of meaning generates psychological momentum. Lives previously guided by pain and fear, suddenly develop a sense of wonder and curiosity.[20] For Zach, the meaning of both events was immediately clear. First, he realized that being a loyal and devoted follower of another's advice could lead him into substantial trouble. Second (as he was able to emancipate from that), he discovered that a deeper guidance was available. As we entertain new meanings, we can sketch a broader story line for our lives, propel ourselves forward, often for no other reason than to find out what happens next. With little discoveries and small successes, curiosity fosters confidence and courage for the Leap—a decision to follow one's heart's desire, regardless of whether it seems practical or even understandable. Zach chose to leave law school—a predetermined path with a precise progression and a good likelihood of material success—

for the "pathless path"—a world of infinite possibility, whose direction was ambiguous and, at least in its early stages, often chosen from one moment to the next.

Zach completed his coursework, and he felt ripe for another adventure. He had never been to the West Coast and his only exposure came through the media, who portrayed its character as exotic and wild. He packed his car and left for San Francisco. It seemed that people throughout the world were flocking there and many had embarked on a similar pilgrimage. They weren't sure exactly what they were looking for, but they seemed to recognize each other as diverse members of the same nomadic family. One of them gave Zach a book with a curious title: *I Seem to Be a Verb*. A year later, Zach would begin an apprenticeship with the author and it would become the most formative and influential relationship of his life.

> The book was written by Buckminster Fuller, and it blew my mind! He wrote, "Man was born with feet, not roots." Now, that may not sound like much, but I was from a very big family, very, very rooted. My mother's side from Poland and my father's from Russia, and they were the first generation. So it was a big family, all the good and bad; a lot of tradition, and it was very safe and secure. Why would anyone leave that? Well, I was feeling suffocated. I had always been a reflection of someone else: his son, her brother, his cousin, and I couldn't get a sense of who *I* was. So I found the book, or rather, it found me!

Fuller's sentences seemed written just for him, and Zach felt the desire to explore this one thing, with his whole being. Synchronistically, upon crossing a street one afternoon, he happened to spy a poster announcing a lecture to be given by Buckminster Fuller later that week.

I was reading Bucky's book, and talking to a lot of people about it. He was giving a talk at San Francisco State, which was quite a political hotbed at the time. So we all trooped over there. I thought there'd be a few hundred people at the most. I really didn't know a lot about him yet. We arrived early, and there were already thousands of people waiting. There were so many that they had to set up loud-speakers outside the big auditorium. It was an incredible scene. People everywhere—music, dancing, people excited —all this energy!

He viewed the Earth not so much as a planet, but as an enormous ship propelled through space. Human beings were not simply inhabitants, but voyagers embarked on a cosmic journey of discovery. In a country divided by the war and paralyzed by its carnage, the sense of freedom and limitless possibility was intoxicating. And Bucky seemed to substantiate everything he said with an intricate and innovative science. He would preach that the Earth's preservation was our crucible and sacred responsibility, and to that end, dedicated his life to the development of architecture and the invention of machines that were both mechanically revolutionary and ecologically benign.

Buckminster Fuller was born in 1895. The afternoon of his talk, he was seventy-six years old and stood barely five feet tall. As he faced his youthful throng, he seemed to transcend the dimensions of age and size, and his words inspired and embraced them. He addressed a generation who doubted they would even realize a future as the war in Vietnam served to only reinforce the dread of having grown up under the nuclear threat. To this subculture, Fuller spoke passionately and precisely to their destiny and the possibility of a very different tomorrow. His pragmatics stood in such stark contrast to the confabulatory rhetoric of political leaders that the young adopted him as their trusted mentor and guide.

> And there was this little guy who just filled the space up all around him. He really talked to who we were, and what was possible. He spoke to us about what our mission on this planet was. I remember thinking, *The Bible is still being written, and this man is a prophet.* I imagined that, if I was listening to a prophet, this is what he would sound like. The talk was three and a half hours long, and he kept weaving in and out of mathematics, social problems, environmental sustainability, geodesic structures. . . . A number of times I thought he had just lost it completely; you know, he was almost eighty, and he was probably going senile right there! But then he'd complete this gigantic weaving of themes, and he'd do this over and over again, and we just became mesmerized. The whole place was mesmerized. Not one person left. No one spoke. At the end, he built to this amazing crescendo, and then he said, "And what it's about is youth, truth, and love," and the place exploded! It was a cosmic experience. I was truly transported.

His technical flights were yet beyond Zach's understanding, but in Bucky's words he could hear the message of optimism and purpose, and Zach knew at that moment that their paths would cross.

> Bucky was a seeker. As much as he knew, he kept exploring, and that's what affected me so deeply. I met his grandson, and he introduced me to Bucky. You know, he was an old man at the time, relatively speaking, but he was not old by any standards I had grown up with. He was so *alive!* Time and again, he would say to me: "Do your *own* thinking!" He didn't want to be anyone's guru. He believed that it was the little individual that makes the ultimate difference. That resonated in me. His grandson and I formed a partnership, and together we scheduled Buckminster Fuller public events throughout the United States. I worked as the hands-on pro-

ducer for eight years—arranging dates, coordinating travel, accompanying Bucky to and fro, and best of all, having daily discussions with him about events, projects, his theories, and his inventions. I worked closely with him up until the time he passed away. In fact, I had the last meeting with him before he died.

When meaning finds its mate in purpose, a powerful off-spring is born. Meaning introduces the idea of connection. The events of our lives, however disparate, are connected through their relevance to our personal and spiritual growth, and as we recognize this, we may become aware that like individual trib-utaries discovering their common course to the ocean, our lives are part of a much deeper current, and more universal evolution of life on the planet. Purpose, then, organizes the data of mean-ing into a teleological frame, and points us toward a future we may never have anticipated or previously understood. At this point, a sense of destiny is born.

Most powerful for me, we worked together on the Hunger Project. Bucky was the first to document scientifically that there were enough resources on the planet to feed every human being. Up until that point, the collective assumption was that there wasn't enough food to go around, and there-fore people had to starve. The intention of the Hunger Project was to make his research known, in as wide a sphere as possible. We knew that if we could broadcast it, we could make it a reality, and it could break the unconsciousness, the cycle of misinformation, and sense of inevitability that sur-rounded it. I also knew Werner Erhard by that time, and despite his more questionable aspects, I had an intuition that, if we could combine Bucky's thinking genius with Werner's organizational genius, we could be very successful.

There were many ups and downs, but the Hunger Project became my mission. It took some time for the two of them to meet, but right off the bat they had a deep connection around the project. The Hunger Project was publicized, and most important, more accurate information about hunger was beginning to make its way into higher and more powerful circles. We began in 1976, and by 1990, a relatively short time, the United Nations acknowledged that there was enough food and enough resources, and that it was really just a matter of whether we, as humanity, have the will to make it work for everybody. I consider this one of the great blessings and successes of my life.

The years flew by. Wiser and more experienced, he continued to practice the lessons he learned through his early encounters with the unexpected. It was not always an easy life, and the route was rarely linear. Yet, the decisions made bore a stamp that was undeniably his.

I learned that it's OK not to know, and to trust the spirit: trust that we are being guided, and our best response is to be open and listen. I've done lots of different things. I've had successful businesses and some failed businesses. I've been a video producer, a production executive, and a concert promoter. I've been an organizational consultant now for many years, and I could give you a whole list of other things I've done. But they were always a means to an end. Always. I've gone through times thinking about if I was a lawyer now: if I married my fiancée, had two cars, our 2.5 kids, our big house in the suburbs, which was already being picked out. You know, wouldn't that have been a hell of a lot easier than being where I was, not knowing, not having a job sometimes? In moments of doubt, I'd say to myself, "Are you crazy?" I'd ask it especially during the painful times, the breakups, and the illnesses. But I could not see that there was any other journey to be on for me than this one. When I'd look at others, I'd ask myself, "Do I want to be doing what they're doing?" And I'd always answer, "No." You know, going back to school, becoming a professional, making a lot of money, it never quite rang true for me. What *was* true for me is that I would do what I need to, to stay in the game, but my priority would always be exploring spirituality and discovering, as best I could, the Truth. It's that way now, and it's been that way, since I felt the light in my apartment, twenty-nine years ago.

An authentic passage is one that burrows into the deepest recesses of one's heart and mind. The demons we encounter may range from the mild to the frightening, but all require the same of us—old patterns of behavior and deeply cherished beliefs must be relinquished. That which has helped to preserve a sense of order and security during everyday life proves of little utility during the Incubation and Search for Meaning. In a very real sense, we need to be emptied in order to become full again—this time with broader context for our lives and an inspired sense of direction. But the passage is not solely an inward journey. At some point, one recognizes the impulse to re-emerge. Interestingly, each person I interviewed completed their tale with a description of their unique attempts to bring what they had learned back into the world.

Zach and I had not spoken for almost two years since our first contact. Recently, when he called, the clarity of his voice with its indelible enthusiasm immediately brought back the delight of our initial interview. As he apprised me of new developments since we'd met, I was aware that Zach continues to be an indefatigable explorer. As a spin-off to their consulting work, he and his wife have created a series of educational programs that specifically offer leadership training for women in positions of power. To date, their seminars have been attended by executives, politicians, professionals, and community organizers, and although their only advertisement is word of mouth, their trainings have been filling for more than a year.

We are working with women throughout the country to discover deeper levels of their own leadership capacities and
what that means to them. It's not about helping them better
cope in a man's world but actually unearthing their own
feminine power and authority at a deeper level, so they may
feel more empowered in their entire lives—in work, yes,
but also in their relationships and with their children. Em-
powering women's leadership, as a man, is a very important
facet of my life now.

I could hear the excitement in his voice as he described
both their new venture and the positive reception it has received, but Zach seemed most moved as he provided some
additional details about his mentor. I am always intrigued with
the beginnings and endings of interviews. If we listen closely at
the edges, we can hear in them the whole tale. Confucius is
reported to have said: "Pay attention to beginnings." Perhaps
he knew that how we start and finish a story can reveal as much
about one's true character and the quality of one's heart as the
details themselves.

Bucky and his wife had been bonded for life. He was deeply
in love with her and had made her a promise. When they
were ready, he would go first. The unspoken was that he
believed his love was so strong that he would be there to
help her on the other side. The last few days of Ann's life,
she had fallen into a coma, and he would visit the hospital
several times a day. He was still quite active and healthy,
but, on the day before she died, he was standing at her
bedside, holding her hand, and he had a massive heart attack
and died. Thirty-six hours later she died as well.

I wondered why Zach was relating, like a parable, this part
of Buckminster Fuller's life. Perhaps I should have asked him,
but I believe I knew. No longer a young man charting his way
alone, Zach, entering his fiftieth year, was deeply devoted to

his wife and partner. As he looked into the future, at the image of his own mortality, the measure of a life well lived seemed dependent not on how much one has accomplished, but on how well one has loved.

> I mean, who's to know what's really going on here? Bucky was always demonstrating unbelievable things. But what I knew was that love was always more important to Bucky than his work. And further, it was love that *fueled* his work, whether it was designing or inventing, teaching or preaching. I believe he made a choice and kept his word. I don't think it was an accident. Bucky was a passionate man with an incredible mind, but an even more incredible heart. Being with him was one of the great joys of my life.

FIVE

THE LEAP

"Which is harder: to be executed, or to suffer that prolonged agony which consists in being trampled to death by geese?"
—SØREN KIERKEGAARD, *Journals*

RADICAL DECISIONS and dramatic changes often follow the Incubation period. Something brewing under the surface finally pokes through into the light of day. The journey of awakening has been a serpentine one, filled with oblique messages and abstruse symbols, but it carries an imperative that, by this point, is very difficult to deny. It is here—after one experiences the Call, survives the vertigo of identity dissolution (so characteristic of the liminal passage), and ascribes it meaning—that many people make unconventional decisions. They may seem questionable, perhaps even inadvisable to those judging from the outside, but these decisions make perfect sense from within.

Tara left the first stable employment she had ever enjoyed and moved her entire family to a small town in the high desert of southern Colorado. Zach eschewed probable status and wealth, and similarly, Jordan left the secure world of traditional science to enter one more ambiguous and controversial. A number of times in his life, Christopher left lucrative and influential positions, choosing instead forms of service that were more directly grass roots and personal. As Joseph Campbell states: "There must always remain, however, from the standpoint of normal waking consciousness, a certain baffling inconsistency between the wisdom brought forth from the deep, and the prudence usually found to be effective in the light world."[1]

I've chosen Charlotte's story as our last, for it not only exemplifies the courage necessary to take creative and unconventional action, but it so completely illustrates all the Stages of Transformation. Her experiences were startling, but so, as we shall hear, were her responses to them. Rather than offering one tale, or even two, Charlotte recounts many. Her life, and sometimes her very survival, has required a prolonged and progressively refined sensitivity—to the unexpected, to its meaning, and to the kind of action it was necessary to take in response.

Charlotte

JESUS AND THE GYM

Charlotte offered to meet me at my office in San Francisco. Still fairly new to the Bay Area, she welcomed the opportunity of spending the day exploring the city. A woman in her mid-fifties, Charlotte gave us a story that provides a detailed portrait of not one, but a progression of events that span nearly twenty years. Comfortably dressed in a tan loose-knit sweater and jeans, she spent nearly three hours relating the most essential portions of her tale directly, without the need for embellishment. They were powerful enough on their own. Charlotte seemed relaxed and well spoken, and she enjoyed the opportunity to talk at length and hear how each story fit in the larger context of her life's journey. Hers is a welcoming visage that conveys a simple warmth, but I was most drawn to her eyes, for as she spoke they seemed to cautiously invite me deeper, not only into the wonder and gratitude she felt in relation to her experiences, but also into the pain and fatigue she has felt during her passages through the unknown.

Each of Charlotte's stories reflects the steps in a journey that took place over many years. Each episode spoke to her in its own language, about both her current life at the time and the possibilities for the future that she would have never considered. Through the years, the unexpected issued more urgent messages; some that required swift and declarative action on her part to avoid danger.

> When I look back over them, the experiences I have had seem to come at times of transition. Many, many times, where there was, if not a dead end, then certainly a tremendous amount of difficulty and pain. These experiences would sort of pop out of nowhere. I mean, they were so beyond my framework. They'd really jangle me and then provide just the kind of opening I needed to make other choices.

Charlotte's first encounter with the unexpected was mild, but compelling. It occurred in her mid-thirties. Recently divorced, Charlotte had begun to create a new home for her four children. For the most part, the kids weathered the transition admirably, settling as best they could into a routine of home life with only one parent. It was hard not seeing their father, who distanced himself from the family, but the decrease in the tension at home was a welcomed relief. A few months after the divorce, however, Charlotte noticed that Sarah, her ten-year-old, was having a difficult time.

> She began to go pretty deep inside herself. She was OK in school, but she'd come home in the afternoon and sit in front of the television, not talk to anyone . . . and just doodle. She became more and more withdrawn. Each day after school, she'd get out pieces of paper and doodle! After a while, I began to nestle close to her to watch what she was drawing.

Charlotte was a trained psychotherapist. She possessed an astute power of observation and a gift in translating what she sensed into language that clients could readily understand and be inspired by. Charlotte felt confident that once she saw Sarah's drawings, she would gain access to the tender heart underneath that needed her mother's love.

> She was drawing floor plans of houses! And each day, it seemed, they got more and more elaborate. Soon she was doing simple interiors, then two-story structures, and then outside landscaping! And they continued to become more detailed as she continued. She didn't seem to be impressed with them at all. She'd just throw it on the floor and start again. It was wild. I got very intrigued with this, because she was still just a child.

Charlotte began to fashion psychological interpretations for Sarah's preoccupation. Their home had been broken apart and now one of its most important members was gone. "Could this be Sarah's way of symbolically repairing the damage?" she wondered. "And could her drawings be an attempt at self-healing by creating a new house; one that she's more in control of?" Charlotte also knew from her training that the house is a classic dream symbol for the psyche, so it only made sense that the drawings reflected Sarah's state of mind. She didn't anticipate, however, the response she would get from a friend to whom she showed the drawings.

> He was a professor at the architecture school at Harvard. I rolled up more than a year's worth of drawings and asked him to look at them. His job kept him very busy, but he called back almost immediately. And he was very startled. He said, "These are better drawings than my first-year students make." And then he said, "What's really weird is that they are drawn exactly to scale!" What was even more bizarre was that she didn't even use a ruler. She was just doodling!

Boston had always been a hub for free thinkers, spiritual seekers, and pharmacological adventurers who explored exotic states of mind. There were many possible explanations for Sarah's proclivity, but none that Charlotte felt confident in. It was probably a result of psychological stress, but that didn't begin to explain her talent. Besides, Sarah had begun to perk up over the year, and she appeared happier and more outgoing again. And she continued to draw. Some friends who were studying mystical traditions suggested that it could be a residue from a past life, but that was something Charlotte knew little about. The only thing really clear to Charlotte was that it surely couldn't have come from her ex-husband or herself.

> He was a schoolteacher and never did anything like this, and I have no technical drawing skills. I truly didn't understand some of the complexity in Sarah's designs. And there were no architects, landscape or otherwise, in our family at all!

As time passed, Charlotte realized that her Search for Meaning in the drawings had been too confined to Sarah and whatever emotional stress she might have been feeling. Perhaps the greater import was for Charlotte, herself, as a parent.

> It was a gentle expansion of perspective, but it was one that made a strong impression on me. It made me look at my children differently. I began to see them as people who were coming *through* me, as opposed to from me. I realized that as they grew up, there were things that were difficult for them, and some of them I contributed to and some I had nothing to do with.

> I began to look at each of my children . . . who they were before, who they are now, and what do they really need and who I am to them. On a very deep level, it transformed my experience of being a parent. I stopped feeling totally responsible for them. I was still their primary emotional and financial support, but something had shifted. I realized I was just one actor . . . a very important actor, but not the whole play.

Charlotte could have viewed her daughter's talent as an anomaly within her clan and left it at that. She could have decided that the whole adventure only reflected Sarah's new-found artistic inclinations and enrolled her for further studies. Each would have been a reasonable, if conventional, response. Instead, Charlotte made two novel decisions. First, she decided that Sarah's fixation had meaning beyond the obvious. It was not simply a random occurrence, nor solely about exceptional ability. She decided it *had* to convey some message. Second, Charlotte allowed the experience to move her, to stir her inside, and in that willingness, a different quality of contemplation about her daughter and perhaps the true nature of the parent-child bond arose. As if to reinforce the message, a similar drama was enacted with her son, shortly thereafter.

He had become a real trial as an adolescent. A redneck kid who got into drugs and drinking and gave me a lot of grief. After high school he joined the navy, the atomic part of it. He signed up for four years. About two weeks out of boot camp, I got this letter asking me to send him books on meditation. Normally I would've ignored it, because it would've have been totally out of character. But after the experience with Sarah, I thought about it differently. I was very careful in what I chose, because I sensed that the request was coming from a very deep part of him: a part I didn't know. It turned out that he used the discipline of the navy to turn his life around. He became a vegetarian, continued spiritual practice, and grew into a fine young man. I watched this and said to myself, "This is really fascinating."

The formative lessons in family life continued. Charlotte learned to allow the unexpected to affect her even if she didn't understand at first, and she learned to trust that its deeper meanings would arise. The coup de grâce involved a simple prediction made on an ordinary afternoon.

Sarah and I were driving down Massachusetts Avenue. She was thirteen at the time. It was an average winter day, grim and gray outside. She was sitting next to me in the front seat and said, "Mom, I know what I'm going to do when I grow up." I replied, "Yes, what are you going to do Sarah?" She said, "Well, I have this picture. I'm going to be working in the inner city, with flowers and plants, creating healing environments for poor people." I said, "Oh, that's great." We had never really talked about anything like that. She's thirty-six now, and she lives in the Atlanta. She works for the Atlanta Botanical Gardens as a horticulturist and artist. And she runs programs for inner-city folks and teachers. So I've learned to listen very carefully now when things seem to come out of the blue.

The tutelage Charlotte received from her children would be invaluable during the difficult times ahead. These early experiences were a proving ground. They cemented the conviction that there are hidden layers of meaning and paths beneath the obvious. In subsequent years, Charlotte discovered that following them could literally make the difference between life and death. Like a sequence of scenes in an unfolding drama of escalating severity, Charlotte's next encounter with the unexpected shattered family life, challenged her ability to cope, and defied the application of rational meaning.

> Sarah was raped. She was twenty-one. It was just after my mother died, and my sister's health was failing. She would die a month later. There was a lot of loss. When Sarah was attacked, I went so deep inside; I hit a place in myself I didn't know existed. I came out so angry that I couldn't see straight. I dropped into this place that I'd never experienced before. It was full of rage and enormous energy. Maybe it's the place where mothers pick up cars to save their children. At that moment, I knew there was something terribly wrong with our family and it had to stop.

The silence in my office held both of us immobile for a minute or so. It was painful for Charlotte to tell this part of the story, and I didn't want to disturb her concentration. At the same time, I wanted to know how she came to such an unusual conclusion. From what thought process did she create that particular meaning out of such a detestable circumstance? Interestingly, the description I received was virtually identical to the one Jordan provided concerning the presence of Lois in the church, and Brooke at the café table: It was immediate and visceral. It simply didn't come from normal thinking.

> I just knew it in my bones. I didn't think about it, or even reflect on it. I had gone far inside. When I emerged, the calm at the center of all that rage was the absolute certainty that Sarah had been vulnerable because there was something

wrong with the family fabric. My husband and I had become very polarized. I had plenty of reasons to hate this man, so there was a vacuum there, and for some reason I couldn't rationally explain, that left Sarah at risk. I just knew it, I don't know how, but I knew that this was a sign that this family needed mending.

The disaster bore a strange fruit. The protracted family tension, the loss of her mother and decline of her sister, had devitalized and burdened Charlotte, but in the extremity of this situation, she found a source of strength and willpower that she had never known.

> It felt like I was plugged into a transformer. When I hit that place in myself, I knew I would be capable of doing anything that needed to happen to stop the loss and trauma in my family. I was so enraged and protective that I vowed never to let any harm come to my children again. I felt fearless. I had never felt that way before. It was the place of truth for me; it seemed like my essence, who I really was. I feel proud about that.

Once again, Charlotte was faced with a familiar choice. She could accept the fact that the assault, however abhorrent, was always a possible hazard in a modern metropolitan area. She would respond accordingly—securing the best medical and emotional treatment for Sarah and caring for her through the difficult healing ahead. And although all of that was true, within the vortex of unexpected, something in her said that this event meant more. It was a symbol of something wrong and a sign that an unusual response was required. In all her years as a therapist, she had never heard of anyone making a similar decision, but it was a leap she simply had to make.

> I did something with my ex-husband I never would have done. I marched into the kitchen, picked up the phone, and

called him. Now I wasn't talking to him, hadn't been for some time, and I said, "Stephen, your birthday's next week, your fiftieth. I'm coming. And I'm going to bring any of the children that want to come." He really didn't know what to say, it was so off the wall. He mumbled something like, "Oh. That'd be nice."

The second thing I did was to call a family therapist and ask advice. She said, "Get him into therapy." So when I saw him, I asked, "Are you concerned about what's happened to Sarah?" He said, "Of course." I said, "Good, then we are going to see a therapist." He was still a bit confused, but to his credit, he agreed.

It was the Braille method. Charlotte was feeling her way along, propelled by her newfound intensity and guided by the meaning she attributed to the family's losses. She had found a therapist who seemed to understand her intentions, and together, they prepared for the first family meeting in years. Consistent with Charlotte's idea of what the family needed, they created a series of therapeutic rituals designed to help each of her children chart their way into late adolescence and adulthood.

It was January first of that year. We were all in New Mexico to scatter the ashes of my sister in her favorite place. The therapist made it clear to the children in a previous session that my ex-husband and I were not meeting to rekindle the marriage but for the well-being of the kids. That afternoon, we all sat on the beds in the hotel room. Stephen and I asked each of them what they needed to move on in their lives. We focused on each one for quite a while. It was very powerful, and they were very frank. We told them to think about this deeply, and then we'd all meet again. Nine months later, we met with the therapist. The first thing she did was tell me to shut up and go sit in the corner. The kids then had to deal with their father and reconnect on their own terms. For the first time in almost twenty years, I was out of the middle. It was wonderful!

It took some time, but Charlotte's resolve to unify her family, if not under one roof but in spirit, reaped success. The family encircled Sarah during her recovery, and with her mother and father united in concern, she was able to find a reservoir of resilience. In a curious way, though, it seemed as if they were not just protecting Sarah. In coming together, the family realized a powerful and protective caring for each member. They felt they were actually healing each other and then bidding each other well on their journey into the next phase of life.

Charlotte had followed her own counsel, even when she knew from the outside her behavior looked strange, and she was more than satisfied with the results. Although she and her ex-husband never remarried, they had become friends. More important, they learned to coordinate their efforts to offer consistent support to the children. The rent in the family fabric had been mended, and each child left home healed, confident, and ready for adventure. From start to finish, eleven years elapsed between the divorce and when the last of the children left home.

The lessons learned during the experience of the Leap tend to generalize, and their influence is progressively integrated into daily life. The impact of their iconoclastic family therapy prompted Charlotte to study that specialty. During the time of her family's repair, she tutored with some of the most accomplished therapists in the country, many of whom lived in the Northeast. It seemed that her career growth paralleled that of her family, and as she approached her late forties, her practice blossomed, and she became a well-known therapist for families in need. Free of household responsibilities for the first time in her adult life, Charlotte assumed the mantle of a full-time professional. She worked long hours and felt happy doing so. It wasn't until a few more years had passed, when she crested fifty, that she recognized how desperately fatigued she had become.

> The kids were gone, and all that family work had ended. I really needed to attend to a shift that needed to happen in me. I began to ask, "OK, what about me? What is my true purpose? What am I going to do with me?" I was tired. You know, I had been running pretty intensely for a long time. I was twenty-one when I had four kids, and now I was fifty-two.

> I realized that I had been struggling for a long time with this underlying sadness. And I could mobilize for my children, and others, but suddenly I knew I had to do this for myself. Make some changes on my own behalf. And this was a whole other thing!

It had been a long time since Charlotte took a vacation. The idea seemed preposterous during the times surrounding the family crises, and thereafter, she powered ahead, giving little thought to her own rest and restoration. But Charlotte began to feel enervated by the constant activity her professional life generated. She was proud of her capacity to raise a family as a single parent, and she had come to enjoy the financial rewards due an accomplished therapist, but to her surprise and alarm, she found herself wondering if she really wanted to continue. Charlotte had lost her bearing, and in honest moments, she had to admit she had little idea in what direction to proceed.

Charlotte and a friend decided to splurge and take a vacation in an exotic locale. She was expecting lots of rest. Some clarity about her life wouldn't be too bad a prize either. Charlotte never expected, however, the arresting vision that would alter the course of her life.

I went with a friend to a mineral springs in New Mexico. Ojo Caliente is a beautiful place. Clean air. Hot sun. Quiet. We went for the express purpose of resting, meditating, and talking about our sense of our life purpose.

So, on the very first day, I'm sitting in the sun. I've got my eyes shut and a moment later, I'm aware that there are all these Indians around me and three medicine men standing right in front of me. My eyes were closed, but this wasn't some ordinary daydream. Everything was so vivid and clear. The medicine men stepped forward and one of them said, "You must ride on the back of the eagle." And then they disappeared.

Charlotte still had very little experience in the realm of psychic experiences. Once, when her mother was dying, she sensed a beautiful rose-hued mist descend between them. It was calming and seemed to communicate that although her mother had reached the end of her life, everything would be all right. It was just nature reclaiming her own. Charlotte didn't fully understand, but she knew enough to let the event continue and savor its simple beauty. Now, instructed by what seemed like native shaman, she felt no choice but to do the same.

The next moment, I'm flying on the back of an eagle and I'm way up high. I'm *literally* on this eagle. I could feel its feathers, and there was even a smell to him that was very tangible. It was very comforting. It felt wonderful. And that's what was so strange, because what I saw, and what it told me, was so frightening.

The eagle said: "This is your life." We're flying pretty high, and I'm looking down on this long valley in front of me! One half the valley, up to the middle, is molten lava . . . black stone. And we're right over it, looking down, and there's a beach. Then, the eagle says, "Look at the beach." And I look, and I can see myself on the beach. I'm sort of this bag of bones that has crawled out onto the beach and I'm barely alive. I'm lying there, charred, almost dead, like a corpse. I'm moving a little bit, but it was clear that I was unable to continue. At the same time, there are these beings, like angels, and they appear to be building a fence behind me, so that I cannot go back. I'm sitting on the eagle, watching this, and all of a sudden, out of the water, come all these little animals!

Beavers and otters, and they begin to build a raft, and then float it on one of the byways. The whole scene was wild! And then the eagle says: "You must surrender totally." Somehow, I understood I would have to lie on the raft and let it take me where it would.

The eagle's voice was matter-of-fact, even comforting, despite its foreboding message, and Charlotte was able to discern the meaning immediately.

I was being shown a death scene, a death vision. It was *my* death! My skin was black, badly burned. I was clearly on my way out. I felt I was being shown a choice: that I could either continue as I was and this would be the consequence, or I could let go—allow myself to surrender to wherever I would float, wherever I might be guided. It was very clear. "If you want to live, this is your next step: Surrender." You know, my mother died of cancer, and so did my sister, and I knew the vision was just showing me that I'd be next. I opened my eyes and felt this strange mix: I felt calm but also shaken. I turned to my friend and said, "Lord, what do I do with this?"

The vision ended as suddenly as it began. Like most callings, the images comprised a curious fusion of the familiar and the fantastic. Charlotte had never studied Native American traditions and had never experienced a lucid vision such as this. At the same time, she knew that the dying figure on the beach was unequivocally her. The power of these elements combined rendered the meaning apparent and her response clear.

> I had a full-time private practice in Boston. I had built it over seventeen years. I understood that I had to close it down and make some radical changes if I were to survive. I needed to take time out, and go wherever I was guided.

The vision and the flight were astonishing. Deep within, she knew its veracity and the wisdom of its counsel. Upon her return, Charlotte began to scale down her practice. Rather than helping to ease the strain, however, she found her health unraveling further, both physically and emotionally. She attempted to translate the vision into action but discovered that the details were thin. It was as if the paint-by-numbers numbers had faded, leaving her with little sense of how to complete the picture.

> I had reached menopause. It hit really hard and there was some deep, deep depression. Nothing was helping much. I was taking some medication. I was trying to exercise. It all helped, but just a little. To make things worse, my back had gone out and I was in severe pain. I would think about the vision, and how it was telling me I was really on my way out. That I was really dying.

The light in New England had grown pale as it does in late December. Most days were cold, and, mixed with the moisture the wind carried from the sea, the chill penetrated nearly any garment one could wear for protection. Charlotte's health continued to fail, and after nearly nine months of chronic pain, she felt withered and frail. Friends were concerned and offered a suggestion they had learned through an experience with the esoteric Islamic practices of the Sufi tradition. It purported to illuminate the present and predict the future, and it seemed exactly what Charlotte needed.

It's called a Dream Incubation. It's done around the New Year. To do it, you begin watching your dreams from the twenty-fifth of December to the fifth of January. The dreams you get for those twelve days each represent a month of the year, so that by the twelfth day, you get a paradigm of the theme for the year. Supposedly, the twenty-fifth, -sixth, and -seventh would correspond to what's happening in January, February, and March, so I thought it would be a good idea.

By now, Charlotte was more experienced in the subterranean realms of the unknown, and in creating the sanctuary necessary for the cultivation of deeper awareness. There was little work for her so near the holidays, so she closed her office and headed south, to Croton-on-Hudson, a small village cradled by the legendary river.

Some friends invited me to stay, so I arrived on Christmas Eve. I decided that later that night, I would ask for a dream that would speak to the whole year; sort of get warmed up for the Incubation.

Charlotte felt freer at the outset of her short junket than she had in a while. She fashioned an intention for the trip that hopefully would speak to her future, and as in the Sufi expression, *Hum de lai la!*—roughly translated, "You take it, Lord" —Charlotte felt she had at least temporarily given her burdens to a higher power. That her back seemed looser helped considerably, and she decided to get some physical exercise before the ambitious feast that was planned.

I had some time to kill before dinner, and since my body was feeling a bit better that day, I decided to go to their gym and ride the bicycle. So I'm in the health club riding the bike and watching everyone walk around, preening, flirting, doing this and that. You know what health clubs are like. And I'm just trying to do my thing. Now, I should tell you that I was brought up in a Presbyterian Congregational family. We weren't religious. I never went to Sunday school and I don't have connections with the Holy Trinity or anything in that arena.

So, I'm riding the bike, working up a sweat, and I happen to look up, and see . . . Jesus! He's standing in front of me, calmly standing there!

Amid the clanging of barbells and the whirring of ski machines stood the Son of God, implacably watching one of his flock. At least the eagle vision occurred in the mountains of the Southwest, where things of that sort presumably happen. But although it *was* Christmas Eve, a vision like this in a health club seemed surreal.

The words just leaped up from inside me, "Oh, my God, not *you!*" I was scared. I was *so* scared! I mean, it was so out of context. Totally unexpected. I remember wondering, *Am I going crazy? Am I forgetting something? Do we have a relationship?* So I just bury my head and close my eyes, and I'm pedaling faster and faster, and I'm thinking, *When I open my eyes, he'll be gone.* And I open my eyes, and he's still there! I start saying under my breath, "Will you please go away?" but he didn't.

He waited and he waited, and it didn't matter how many times I closed my eyes. He remained in the same spot. I looked to see if maybe it was a picture on the wall, but, you know, health clubs don't normally *have* pictures of Jesus opposite the stationary bikes! Finally, I thought, *He's not going away, so he clearly wants to talk to me.* So I calmed myself a bit and looked at him and he started to talk to me. He said, "You must move an hour a day. A new energy is coming onto the planet. It is coming into the physical body to integrate body, mind, and emotions. The integration can only happen in movement." And then he was gone.

A simple visit to the health club turned into a spiritual encounter, and it left her befuddled. Driving back, she ran the event through her mind again and again. Charlotte could sense the dual nature of the message. Spoken in universal tones, it could apply to almost everyone she knew. But the vision also seemed to speak directly to her—to her physical problems and her depression.

> It felt generic but also very personal. Truthfully, I just didn't know what to do with it. I went back for dinner, and although I'm very close with my friends, I didn't tell them. I was just so stunned. I carried on normal conversation at dinner, I'm not sure how, and then I went straight to bed.

The advice seemed clear enough. She could appreciate its inherent wisdom and common sense, and she would probably follow it. But then there was the matter of *who* was speaking to her. Though in her thirties, forties, and now early fifties she studied the perennial teachings from many spiritual traditions, she had assiduously avoided Jesus. The dogma of the church and its patriarchal posture never spoke to her, and she had witnessed firsthand the confusion it generated in both friends and clients. Thinking about it, she was hard-pressed to identify any other deity whose sudden presence in her life would surprise her more. Once again, Charlotte found herself in liminal territory. Later that night, as if to accentuate her vision, she had a series of dreams, seven[2] in all, with the same scene appearing in each one.

> I'm standing in a totally dark space, totally black. It's a small room, and I know it's a small room, but it feels fine. It feels like I'm standing in the darkness of the feminine. It wasn't dark-scary. It was comfortable, like I was being held there;

soft, warm, and womblike. The only thing that I could see was this extraordinary piece of stained glass on the wall. It was of Jesus. And he spoke to me out of the picture.

He said, "I was born in human form 2,000 years ago, that man might know of my existence, and that seeded the next 2,000 years. I'm being born this Christmas in every man and woman's heart, that they may know the love that I am. This will seed the next 2,000 years." That was it.

There was a long pause. Charlotte seemed to be listening to the words he'd just spoken, as if hearing them again brought her back to a sacred place. In fact, she returned to the dream often, like a small pilgrimage or the touching of a sacred stone.

I took it very seriously. Both the vision and the dream. I began to do at least an hour of exercise a day, and I believe it saved my life. I was going downhill so fast at that point. The dream: Well, it tapped into a level of the unconscious I'd never been in. I believe it was a call to me to honor the feminine and strengthen it. The dream was saying Jesus would appear in every man *and* woman's heart. And you know, as a woman, I've always felt out of context, less than, and it was a message that that wasn't gonna be true anymore. It felt like a call for me, and women as a whole, to be equal. So it was a personal and collective message. It certainly popped me out of any passivity I had left in me.

Charlotte returned from her trip and decided to tell a few trusted friends of her experience. To her relief, they responded in kind—believing she had received a Call, perhaps from Jesus, and certainly from the deepest recesses of her soul. Charlotte knew herself. She knew that hers would not be a traditional, or even culturally recognizable, relationship with Jesus. She joined a Congregational Church, one as free of trappings as she could find, so she might continue to surround herself with people drawn to Jesus, but mostly, she meditated on the dream and the qualities of Jesus she was familiar with. Over time, Charlotte began to feel a private and personal bond develop. Her health began to improve, and she knew the time had drawn near for her to leave her practice and the city in which she'd lived for most of her life.

> I remember going back to my friend's house the next Christmas. I was walking uphill, longing for that connection again, and I realized that it was time to move and reorient my life. I had begun to get well. The combination of the vision and the dream gave me the courage to trust the guidance I was receiving in my meditations. I mean, to the rational mind, it looked totally insane to shut my practice at my age and move across the country. But that's what I did. About six years ago now, I left Boston with whatever I could fit in my car.

Loneliness is a part of the journey. No one can live our lives for us. The support of family and friends can help, but that doesn't negate the fact that we go through these passages alone. The Call propels us into liminal space. Swirling within its ambiguity, our aloneness is most keenly felt. Everything is new and odd, and moments of doubt are inevitable. Yet, as I've described, another reality parallels this one. As much as people report feelings of aloneness, they also recount the experience of a connection deeper and more profound than ever before. It is felt personally, but it does not come from another individual. It is practical to this world, but seems to come from beyond. This connection is so powerful that common loneliness and isolation are often dissolved.

The pull to re-create her clinical practice on the West Coast was strong at first. The Bay Area had become a center for training in family therapy, and Charlotte knew she could be successful. But she had to admit it would really be an attempt to assuage the aloneness she felt, to somehow replicate the familiarity of her former home and alleviate the understandable apprehension she felt concerning the sea change ahead. But deep within, Charlotte knew something was different. Charlotte had little desire to provide long-term psychotherapy. No longer interested in client loads or managed care, Charlotte wanted to devote most of her time to her physical healing and a relationship to the sacred. For income, Charlotte took a part-time job as a therapist at a local hospital. The remainder of the time, she spent walking the hills surrounding the Bay, meditating, and letting her body rest.

It had been a long journey. From her young daughter's first drawings to her exodus from the East Coast, nearly thirty years had passed. She had literally witnessed death and resurrection, and it left her feeling wiser and lighter than she had in many years. Charlotte was still a comparatively young woman. Now that her body was becoming strong again, she was confident and expectant and looked forward to her future adventures.

I attempted to contact Charlotte this past Thanksgiving holiday. The phone number of two years ago was still hers, but the message informed that she was vacationing in northern California and wouldn't be back for a week. Somehow, I imagined her on walks through streambeds and overgrown trails, and resting, enjoying contemplative time in her own company. She called a week later, to offer an update, and she sent a brochure describing her new line of work. It read, "Life Purpose Counseling: Designed to help negotiate life's challenges with independence, self-esteem, and dignity."

EPILOGUE

THE INTEGRATION

"Here is the great key . . . the two kingdoms are actually one. The realm of the Gods is a forgotten dimension of the world we know. The exploration of that dimension is the whole sense of the deed of the hero."[1]

—JOSEPH CAMPBELL

IT CAN TAKE a lifetime to truly integrate the experiences of both the unexpected and the liminal world. (In some forms of Zen ordination, the priest is forbidden to function as a cleric for ten years. During that time, he or she is expected to live the teachings as an "ordinary" citizen and learn to integrate the practices into ordinary life. Having done that, he or she is considered qualified.) In a celebrated example of integration, Black Elk, of the Lakota tribe, returned from a series of visions on Harney Peak, the center of the world for the Ogala Sioux. Only a boy of nine, he found reentry difficult, and it lasted many years. He was afraid to speak of his experience, even to his closest relatives, but something was visible to the trained eye:

> Whirlwind Chaser [a local medicine man] sat down and looked at me for a long time and then he said to my father: "Your boy there is sitting in a sacred manner. I do not know what it is, but there is something special for him to do, for just as I came in I could see a power like a light all through his body."[2]

Eight years after his vision, when Black Elk was still only seventeen years old, he was rescued from virtual insanity by neighboring tribal elders, who helped him bring his experience back to the earth. The elders learned the songs Black Elk heard and enacted the visions he saw. The transition was complete, for in a very real way, the two worlds had become connected. Over time, Black Elk would return to his vision for inspiration and guidance, and in doing so, begin to realize his destiny as a great medicine man of his people.

We have come a long way. We have been privy to extraordinary journeys, made by people who chose to view their excursions into the unexpected as, in the words of Kurt Vonnegut, "dancing lessons from God." The stories in *Crossings* demonstrate the life-transforming potential of an encounter with the unusual. Even when specific understanding was not yet forthcoming, those interviewed here chose to believe that a dialogue with a greater or deeper source had occurred. This choice acts as a precise key to a precise lock on a particular door. We enjoy absolute freedom here. We may see the progression of our lives as the collection of random events that arise capriciously and bear little relation to one another. The chronicle of our lives is then written, like the Farmer's Almanac, as a compendium of interesting, sometimes fascinating occurrences, linked, for most part, by date and time.

Alternately, we can choose to meet the unexpected with curiosity and wonder. We can devote ourselves to comprehending its deepest meaning and intuiting the best possible response from the deepest part of ourselves. The effects of this choice are dramatic. A sense of adventure is kindled. An atmosphere of intrigue infuses our days. Life is experienced, not as the rote succession of minutes and hours, but as the unfolding of a great mystery, and the inauguration of a great quest. Inner resources are brought to bear that may have lain dormant for years, and where boredom, or depression, or just a faint sense of the sameness of life had once encamped within us, we awaken. (I have witnessed this scenario more times than I can count in psychotherapy. Often, patients are not so much "cured," as having discovered a broader, more spiritually meaningful context that supplants itself in the center of their lives. Then, rather than feeling victimized by the assortment of random symptoms to which they had succumbed, they experience themselves on a quest that unearths the best in them—their courage, vision, and blessedly, a sense of humor.)

Encounters with the unexpected leave a legacy. Those who accept the challenge of this passage, who respond to the unusual (often with unusual choices), have learned to traverse an arcane territory. They have developed a working relationship to the unexpected, and respond with skillfulness as it continues to enter their lives. For once accepted, the journey of awakening never ends, and one's relationship to the unexpected forever deepens.

At the close of these stories, I am reminded of the times of Chaucer, when a pilgrim would be met by the villagers with the salutation, "Tell us the good word!" A fire would be kindled, the townspeople would gather, and a tale would be told. The great myths and legends were passed down this way. They were about encounters with the unusual, and about the courage and resourcefulness brought to bear to meet them. At the end of the tale, as the last firelog smoldered to ash, the people would return to their cottages, their hearts and minds inspired and sated. Through shared stories, all became fellow travelers; co-protagonists on an adventure into the unknown, and witnesses to its capacity to bring out the best of what is human within us.

My last question was always the same. "What is your relationship to the unexpected now?" Although each answered in his or her own way, the responses proved consistent in two respects. First, all agreed that the journey continues. Initial experiences with the unexpected were seen to have opened a door and increased one's sensitivity to these ephemeral realms. Interestingly, most describe continued encounters with the unexpected, often in less dramatic form. As Christopher describes:

> I've had a lot of experiences, as I suppose many people have. I think we all have them. For me, they have become more subtle over time, and they've deepened. I think they are a natural outgrowth of following a spiritual path.

And Catherine:

> I try to be more aware of the less dramatic things now. People's energy, and the way events are unfolding. I notice my dreams more . . . I'm becoming more proficient in interpreting them. I sometimes see letters and words, like typewriter keys in my mind, and these offer information and guidance I wouldn't normally have. A lot of times, I have to unhook my mind, get out of the intellect, and sort of let myself flow along with what is happening. Then it's easier to figure out. It's a funny paradox. The less I try to control things, the more control I feel I have.

Second, what began with a set of responses to a single experience has now evolved into a generalized orientation toward life: a posture of openness to the unusual and a confidence that it carries a message. Through the tutelage of the unexpected, each has crafted his or her own individual style, but, as we can hear, all bear remarkable similarities. Brooke describes the state to which she and Ricardo aspire. As the years pass, they internalize it more and more:

> As much as we can, we live our lives with unconditional love, non-expectation, and no judgment. I mean, we have minds—we plan and have a good capacity for critical judgment when we need it—but for the most part, we leave our eyes wide open and be attentive to signs.

As is his wont, Zach speaks both of pragmatics and ecstatics:

> It's a matter of listening, of going inside both physically and emotionally. Be open to whatever you sense inside, even if you don't understand it at first. It's OK not to know. But listen as deeply as you can.

> I think we all have access to our truth, and if we are really committed to discovering the truth that's within us, the spirit that is within us, whatever you want to call it, then life will turn out good for you. It really will! All we need to do is to be willing to accept that energy inside. If it's a Jewish G-d, then yes! If it's Jesus, yes! If it's the Buddha, yes! We really are children of God. And we really both love and are loved.

Tara has come to expect the unexpected. During our last conversation, she told me two more stories of her grandfather. She believes he has continued to teach her, even after his death. No longer lost and in great pain, Tara is now a woman of considerable insight. For the past nine years she has been the director of an international program for adolescents, providing both indigenous teaching and wilderness leadership training. Her integration of native wisdom and Eastern spirituality has garnered requests to teach at universities throughout the country

as well as to speak at a number of recent global peace conferences. Still, there was a circle to complete, and in two deft
strokes of the unexpected, it was done.

One of the most important things that Grandfather taught
me was how to die. Two things happened. On the night of
his death, I was giving a workshop near Crestone, in the
mountains. I was reached by phone, and I took some time
to go into another room and just sit quietly. I began to cry.
The next moment, when I opened my eyes, he was standing
there looking at me! It was even clearer than the first time.
He said, "Why are you crying? I am not sad, and you
shouldn't be either." Then he said, "Be happy! And sing a
song for me!" And then he was gone. I just had to laugh.
And I sang for a while.

I returned to Taos for the funeral a week later. His daughter
told me she had to speak to me. She felt she should tell me
the story of his last hours, although she didn't know why.
She told me that on his last day, in his hospital room, he
began to sing. He seemed to pass in and out of consciousness,
but he kept singing sacred songs. And he was singing them
loud! The nurses would come in and tell him to stop, beg
him to be quiet, but he just kept on singing. This went on
for hours. Then, toward late afternoon, he suddenly stopped.
His daughter said he had this radiant look on his face, and
he exclaimed, "Here they are! Here they are—my elders
have come for me! And here we go!" And then he died!

You know, I was never totally sure about the vision in my
apartment that day. Despite everything that happened after,
all that seemed to confirm it, there had always been a bit of
doubt. I mean, it was *so* far out there. But this experience
ended my speculation. Not only did he appear to me again,
saying something I never would have thought, but evidently,
his elders appeared to him as well. And just as he came to
take me home, they came for him.

NOTES

INTRODUCTION

1 The story of Karl is found throughout my book *Waking Up, Alive*. This particular episode can be found in the chapter entitled "Opening to the Unexpected" (New York: Putnam, 1994), pp. 225–6.

2 Joseph Campbell, the late mythologist, speaks about the Call to Adventure, reflected in our myths, fables, fairy tales, and lore. Here he provides a context for the extraordinary within the archetype of the quest. He also describes the refusal of the Call—in which "the subject loses the power of significant affirmative action and becomes a victim to be saved. His flowering world becomes a wasteland of dry stones and his life feels meaningless." *The Hero with a Thousand Faces* (New York: Bollingen Foundation, 1949), p. 59.

3 Morris Berman, *The Re-enchantment of the World* (New York: Bantam New Age, 1984), p. 134.

4 Werner Heisenberg, the physicist who pioneered quantum mechanics, has demonstrated that in fact a complete separation of researcher and subject is impossible. Further, he shows that any act of research will unavoidably affect what is being studied. A participatory researcher accepts this and attempts to utilize this inevitable connection to his or her advantage, endeavoring to gain insight through the common experience of being human.

5 These characteristics reported by subjects bear a marked similarity to those observed by Abraham Maslow, father of humanistic psychology, in people he identified as "Self-Actualizers." The characteristics include:
—perceiving reality efficiently and able to tolerate uncertainty
—accepting themselves and others for what they are
—spontaneous in thought and behavior
—problem-centered rather than self-centered
—having a good sense of humor

—highly creative

—resistant to enculturation, although not purposely unconventional

—concerned for the welfare of humanity

—capable of deep appreciation of the basic experiences of life

—able to establish deep, satisfying interpersonal relations with a few rather than many people

—able to look at life from an objective viewpoint (1954, 1967)

6 During my interviews with people for my first book, *Waking Up, Alive!*, it was clear that their experiences also fit within the form of the passage. In a very real sense, people who are suicidal are correct: something needs to die. They possess a mistaken and highly destructive notion, however, that it is *them*. Their suicidiality more often attempts to communicate that what must die may be a constrictive relationship, toxic family interractions, a job that is stultifying, an addictive pattern, or a rigid and limited sense of identity that has smothered enjoyment, a sense of beauty, and an appreciation of the spirit.

7 Jack Kornfield, an Eastern studies major in college, entered monasteries in Burma and Thailand, and Joseph Goldstein took monk's vows in Bodh-Gaya, the historical site of the Buddha's enlightenment. Joseph still lives and teaches on the grounds of the center in Barre, while Jack left in the late 1980s to create a dharma center on the West Coast. This became the Spirit Rock Meditation Center, just north of San Francisco. See Rick Fields, *How The Swans Came to the Lake* (Boston: Shambala, 1991), pp. 320–22.

ONE

1 Job's name has been interpreted by some to mean, "He who turns to God." All Bible references are from the *Standard Revised Version, Harper Study Bible.*

2 Job 1.1-3.

3 *Grimms' Fairy Tales*, "The Frog King."

4 "The World Is Too Much with Us, Late and Soon," from *William Wordsworth, the Poems*, Vol. 1, John O'Hayden (ed.) (New York: Penguin, 1977), p. 568.

5 Roger N. Walsh, *The Spirit of Shamanism* (New York: Tarcher/Putnam, 1990), p. 49.

6 Antoine de Saint-Exupéry, *The Little Prince* (New York: Harcourt Brace, 1974).

7 Victor Frankl, in *Man's Search for Meaning* 4th edition (New York: Beacon Press, 1992), and Bruno Bettleheim, in *Surviving and Other Essays* (New York: Knopf, 1952), both wrote about the power of asking these questions. They independently observed that those who entertained the questions about the ultimate meaning and purpose of their lives were better able to endure extreme hardship and catastrophic circumstance, and emerge from the trauma, shaken perhaps, but psychologically intact and wiser. Their work studied prisoners of concentration camps in WWII to discover why some were able to survive while others, who endured equal physical deprivation, perished.

8 Mahatma Gandhi, *Non-Violence in Peace and War* (New York: Garland Publishing, 1948), p. 77.

TWO

1 A. Eliot, *Universal Myths* (New York: Meridian, 1976), p. 100.

2 J. E. Cirlot, *A Dictionary of Symbols* (New York: Philosophical Library, 1962), p. 342.

3 *Native American Wisdom* edited by K. Berburn, Ph.D., and L. Mengelkoch, M.A. (San Rafael, CA: New World Library, 1991).

4 *From the Sacred Pipe: Black Elk's Account of the Seven Rites of the Ogala Sioux*, recorded and edited by Joseph Epes Brown (Norman, OK: University of Oklahoma Press, 1953), p. 55.

5 J. Campbell, *The Hero with a Thousand Faces*, p. 51.

6 Ibid., p. 53.

7 Ibid., p. 56.

8 Mircea Eliade, one of the great scholars of comparative religion in our time, discussed the symbolism of the Symplegades—the two enormous rocks barring the entrance to the Black Sea. They would clash together intermittently, destroying anything in their jaws, but they remained silent and still when Jason and the Argonauts passed through in the Argo. Eliade writes: "The Symplegades show us the paradoxical nature of passage into the beyond, or, more precisely, of transfer from this world to a world that is transcendent. . . . These mythical images and folklore motifs of the dangerous passage and the paradoxical transfer express the necessity for a change in [one's very] mode of being to attain to the world of

spirit." In *Rites and Symbols of Initiation and Shamanism*, new edition (Dallas: Spring Publications, 1994). Sounding a similar theme, Jungian analyst Jean Shinoda Bolen writes of the symbolism of the Grand Cross in astrology and the necessity to see beyond polarities. As a personal message in negotiating her divorce and the consequent enormously painful transition, the Grand Cross "[symbolized] a time of crisis that would break me if I were to be caught between the opposites; I would be crucified on the Grand Cross unless I grew 'large enough' to contain these opposites within my psyche and my life." In *Crossing to Avalon* (San Francisco: Harper, 1994), p. 108. Both of these in turn provide illustrations of Jung's notion that there exists a psychic energy that engenders the unification of opposites through the creation of symbol. When we are able to embrace both sides, rather than trying to eliminate one or the other, dynamic psychic tension is created that, at some point, engenders a third force, a "transcendent function," which in one insightful stroke brings opposites together, contained within a new form or structure. This unusual psychic force doesn't happen serendipitously. The transcendent function is teleological—it acts with a purpose, to designate a direction through the stuckness, intractable conflicts, and one-sidedness in our lives.

9 The noted anthropologist Victor Turner describes the marriage of these polarities during ritual. He observes that many ritual ceremonies contain two powerful, but opposite, elements. One is abstract and ideal, and the other concrete, somatic, and emotional. In ritual, as these properties are exchanged, the abstract is fused with the concrete so that the abstract becomes grounded and is made personal for everyone in the ceremony, while the particular and somatic pole becomes ennobled and equated with the highest ideas of the collective. In Barbara Meyerhoff's *Number Our Days* (New York: Touchstone, 1978), p. 257.

10 Judith Viorst, *Necessary Losses* (New York: Simon & Schuster, 1986), pp. 249, 252.

11 Sigmund Freud, *Mourning and Melancholia* (London: Hogarth Press, 1917) SE 14, 243–58. In addition, John Bowlby's *Loss* (New York: Basic Books, 1980) provides perhaps the most comprehensive treatment of the psychology of loss, its natural course, and pathological complications.

12 Viorst, *Necessary Losses*, p. 265.

13 This line of thought is part of a discussion in Morris Berman's *The Reenchantment of the World*, p. 131. Here, he argues that rational compre-

hension of our world plays a role only after the immersion into an experience of something new. It's only after we have a visceral experience of something, after we let it deeply affect us, that we begin to conceptualize it, find rationale for it, and create categories in which to place the experience.

14 Eastern religious traditions contribute an important perspective to this question through the concept of karma. Although notions of karma vary slightly from diverse cultural influences, they all express the fundamental conviction that the circumstances of our present life have actually been determined by both actions in previous lives and the particular route or path we must travel in order to develop spiritually. In this sense, the notion of karma and Jung's theory of synchronicity share a teleological orientation—that the events that befall us actually point us in the direction of greater awareness, wholeness, and spiritual attainment.

15 It is true that, during the 1970s through the present, the Transpersonal Psychology Movement has enthusiastically embraced spiritual and parapsychological phenomena. Transpersonal Psychology recognizes the legitimacy of and the power of spiritual experiences to affect powerful psychological healing and change. The movement's greatest achievement, however, rather than representing a unified system of thought that attempts to explain such experiences, has been to provide an institutional umbrella and refuge for a wide variety of theory and technique. A few other approaches that endeavor to embrace both the spiritual and psychological do exist. Roberto Assagioli's Psychosynthesis, Stan Grof's Holotropic Breath Work, and Al Hameed's fusion of Object Relations Theory and Spiritual Thought are examples. To date, however, perhaps no work has as comprehensively addressed "boundary phenomena" as that of Carl Jung. He endeavored throughout his life to understand the intrapsychic conditions that would lead one to be most impacted by external events.

16 In answer to Job, Jung wrestles with the question of an external agency. Ultimately, he concedes, "All we can do is construct models which we know to be inadequate."

17 See Chapter Three.

18 Rabbi Steinsaltz is a teacher, mathematician, chemist, biologist, linguist, sculptor, Biblical zoologist, and the author of books and papers on Jewish philosophy and mysticism. In 1967, he was asked to prepare a new edition of the Babylonian Talmudic Hebrew, with commentary. The

Talmud is a 1,500-year-old repository of rabbinic reflections on the written and oral law. From an interview by Jean Sulzberger, *Parabola* (Spring 1994): 26.

THREE

1 Arnold van Gennep, an early twentieth-century French anthropologist, examined the common elements in the passage rituals of tribal cultures worldwide. He found remarkable consistency despite differences in tribal myths, mores, and specific meaning of the cultural practices. He formulated a model of the passage that has been echoed throughout the century by his predecessors and that bears relevance for understanding the modern man and woman's individual passages, and the unexpected events that herald them. In van Gennep's model, he identifies three stages of the rite of passage: Separation, Transition, and Incorporation. *The Rites of Passage*, translated by Monika Vizedom and Garielle Caffee (London: Routledge & Kegan Paul, 1909).

Mircea Eliade and Victor Turner further investigated commonalities in rituals and practices that underscored the individual differences among people. Eliade, for instance, discovered marked similarities between initiation rituals of the Plains Indians and indigenous groups in Siberia. The process by which young members of the clan were identified as future shaman were remarkably consistent. Even more provocative, however, was her discovery that virtually the same process occurred on the other side of the world, among the Warburton and Arunta tribes in subequatorial Australia.

Eliade observed a two-part structure to rites of passage, of which the initiation rite is perhaps the most potent. The first stage involves a ritual death. Ritual death represents the symbolic retrogression into Chaos, the primal order of the universe, either through ceremonies of dance, drumming and chanting, wandering in the savanna and fasting, or ingesting hallucinogenic plants. For the advent of a new order, the old must be annihilated. Encounters with spirits or demons that force the initiate to relinquish the comforts of childhood and parental protection are common, and visions are offered for future guidance, should the initiate survive his or her ordeal. A renowned medicine man of the Unmatjera tribe in Australia described the experience of ritual death at the hands of the old doctor who had "killed" him by throwing crystals at him with a spear thrower. As anthropologists Spencer and Gillan recount:

> The old [doctor] then cut out all of [the boy's] insides—intestines, liver, heart, lungs—everything, in fact, and left him lying all night long on the ground. In the morning the old man came and looked at him and placed some more atnongara stones (i.e. small crystals) inside his body and in his arms and legs, and covered over his face with leaves. Then he sang over him until his body was all swollen up. When this was so he provided him with a complete set of new inside parts, placed a lot more atnongara stones in him, and patted him on the head, which caused him to jump up alive.

2 The Buriat of Siberia believe that at these times the young man's soul is transported by spirits to the gods, whereupon he is instructed by his shaman ancestors "in the secrets of his profession, the forms and names of the gods, the worship and names of the spirits."

3 Eliade relates the incredible story of a young Eskimo shaman who fell into the icy waters near his village and survived five days in the water. It is told that when he emerged his clothes were still dry.

4 Examples of such behavior include: singing in one's sleep, walking naked into the forest during winter, eating bark, distraction, speaking to spirits, exploding into fits of anger or laughter, and even cutting oneself. In Eliade, *Rites and Symbols of Initiation and Shamanism.*

5 It is not uncommon for months or years to pass as meaning becomes clear.

6 The idea of surrender is an anathema in Western culture and is most often synonymous with defeat. On the whole, we have little understanding and experience with the power and elegance of a posture of yielding, or in the common vernacular, letting go. (Perhaps the closest we come is the Christian mystical notion of spiritual endurance. But for the most part, one must consult Eastern and indigenous cultures for guidance here.) Psychiatrist and analyst Joseph Henderson, in his bountiful and magnificent text, *The Wisdom of the Serpent*, clarifies this point in reference to the rite of initiation. "Initiation is derived from the Latin *in ire*, 'to enter into' and therefore . . . denotes a temporary withdrawal from outer actions, especially adventures of the heroic sort. *Submission* [my italics] is the characteristic of initiation, but it is not apathy or weakness; it contains a strong element of the archetypal 'trial and error' carried over from the heroic phase of life." *Wisdom of the Serpent* (Princeton: Princeton University Press, 1990)

7 St. John's Dark Night of the Soul and the Sumerian myth of Innana descending into Hades, de-boned and hanging on the wall, are stark, but sometimes accurate, reflections of how people feel during the early phase of Incubation. Dreams of losing one's teeth (one's grip), of not knowing where one's home is, and generally feeling lost are also common.

8 Hebrews 11.1.

9 Again, an interesting parallel here to the observations that in various tribes the initiate is covered with mud, the color of earth, upon embarking on the quest. This symbolizes the loss of one's previous identity and the return to Chaos, the state that precedes the creation of form. With respect to the shaman, the psychic Chaos, the strange behaviors and symptoms that predict his or her future role are signs that the "profane man is dissolving and a new personality is being prepared for birth." In Eliade's *Rites and Symbols of Initiation and Shamanism*, p. 89.

10 *Standard Revised Version, Harper Study Bible*, Luke 1.30. An alternative translation given reads, "Blessed are you among women!"

11 Ibid., Luke 1.32.

12 Ibid., Luke 1.33.

13 Ibid., Luke 1.38.

14 Ibid., Luke 1.39.

15 Ibid., Luke 1.41.

16 Elizabeth would have a child. The eighth day after the child's birth was the time of both circumcision and naming, and the family present decided to name the child after the father, Zechariah. Elizabeth, however, to the astonishment of everyone, refused and insisted on the name John. When Zechariah, whose word would customarily be final, was entreated, he wrote the name John on his tablet, whereupon Zechariah's mouth opened, "and his tongue loosed, and he spoke, blessing God" (Luke 1.64). The child was to become John the Baptist.

17 Ibid., Luke 1.45.

18 William Bridges, *Transitions* (Reading, MA: Addison-Wesley, 1980), p. 84.

19 "Quicken" was the word used when spiritual seekers on pilgrimage would enter a holy place and feel themselves stirred and closer to divinity. Sometimes a healing would result, or a vision or deep sense of being touched by God. They would leave changed and more emboldened to pursue a life of spiritual practice.

20 B. Walker, *The Woman's Encyclopedia of Myth and Secrets* (San Francisco: Harper & Row, 1983), pp. 252–53.

21 "The latest incarnation of Oedipus, the continued romance of Beauty and the Beast, stand this afternoon on the corner of 42nd Street and Fifth Avenue, waiting for the traffic light to change." Campbell, *The Hero with a Thousand Faces*, p. 4.

FOUR

1 *Parabola* (Spring 1994): 27.

2 Carl Jung, *Answer to Job* in *Collected Works # 11* (Princeton: Bollingen Series), p. 360.

3 In fact, a major cause of neurosis may lie in our inability to discover meaning in and for our lives. Salvador Maddi in his essay, "The Search for Meaning," opined that neurosis stems "from a comprehensive failure in the search for meaning in life." Further, he posits that a major cognitive component of neurosis is "meaninglessness, or the chronic inability to believe in the truth, importance, usefulness, or interest value of any of the things one is engaged in or can imagine doing." *Nebraska Symposium on Motivation*, 1970 edition edited by W. Arnold and M. Page (Lincoln: University of Nebraska Press, 1970), pp. 137–86, and S. Maddi, "Existential Neurosis" in *Journal of Abnormal Psychology* 72 (1967): 311–25.

4 Carl Jung, *Psychology and the Occult* (Princeton: Princeton University Press, 1977), pp. 136–67.

5 As the stories illustrate, these questions are not simply intellectual ones. They are often prompted by great pain and confusion. Similarly, the answers are not simply intellectual constructions, but hard-won discoveries about the nature of life.

6 *American Heritage Dictionary of English*, p. 1082.

7 *Merriam Webster Collegiate Dictionary*, p. 700.

8 Ibid.

9 Helen Luke was born in 1904 and received her graduate education in French and Italian literature at Oxford. She met Carl Jung in Zurich and became a student, eventually building a psychotherapy practice in Los Angeles, before creating the Apple Farm Community. Her books include *The Way of the Woman, Old Age: Journey into Simplicity*, and *Dark Wood to White Rose: Journey and Transformation in Dante's Divine Comedy*.

10 Merton's true quote: "True prayer is learned in the hour when prayer seems impossible and the heart has turned to stone." In this context, "prayer" and connecting to some greater process can be read as synonymous.

11 Centers for Disease Control, Atlanta, Georgia.

12 Of the remaining Plains Indians, the two largest populations of Lakota (or Sioux) live on the Pine Ridge and the Rosebud Reservations in South Dakota.

13 Victor Turner, *From Ritual to Theater: The Human Seriousness of Play* (New York: PAJ Publications, 1982), p. 26.

14 This project has been led from its inception by Professor Emeritus Dr. Robert G. Jahn. The laboratory manager is Brenda Dunne. A catalog of their work and most recent journal submissions appear on their Web site, accessed through Princeton University.

15 See Robert G. Jahn and Brenda Dunne, *Margins of Reality: The Role of Consciousness in the Physical World* (New York: Harcourt Brace Jovanovich, 1987) for a detailed description of this work, and the collateral research this inspired.

16 In a similar series of experiments, a subject would notify the lab that on, for instance, Monday, she would attempt to influence the number generator, but for a specific period of time, on the following Thursday. On that Thursday, the production of random numbers would be observed to shift as intended. The lab could now conjecture effects in the future. Finally, a subject would notify the lab that she had attempted to skew the production of numbers in the past. In other words, on, for instance, a Monday, a subject would attempt to influence the production of numbers during a certain time from the previous Thursday. To their astonishment, as long as the results of the number production hadn't been looked at (fixed) by a technician on that previous day, results consistently showed a skew in the direction intended by the subject.

17 Campbell, *The Hero with a Thousand Faces*, p. 101.

18 The five-pronged Vajra scepter cuts through the delusions of aggression, pride, passion, jealousy, and ignorance. It does so in ways that are penetrating, fearless, open, and utterly destructive. The scepter has the capacity to cut through these confusions and return us to the experience of basic sanity. From Chogyam Trungpa, *Journey Without a Goal: The Tantric Wisdom of the Buddha* (Boston: Shambala, 1995).

19 In many indigenous cultures, the structure of the psyche and how human

beings matured was understood. To aid that process, rituals of passage were enacted. Jung appreciated how the mythological comes to life during our ordinary days and non-ordinary nights. As Eliade expressed directly:

> Initiation is so closely linked to the mode of being of human existence that a considerable number of modern man's acts and gestures continue to repeat initiatory scenarios. Very often the "struggle for life," the "ordeals" and "difficulties" that stand in the way of a vocation or a career in some sort, reiterate the ordeals of initiation.

Mircea Eliade, *The Sacred and the Profane* (New York: Harcourt Brace Jovanovich, 1957), pp. 208–9.

20 A similar process occurs in successful psychotherapy. Most often, a client's motivation for entering therapy is pain-based. As therapy proceeds, it is curiosity and a desire to know what is true and enduring in life that fuels deeper exploration.

FIVE

1 Campbell, *The Hero with a Thousand Faces*, p. 127.
2 Mythologically, the number seven is most associated with the process of initiation, especially into the realm referred to as "feminine wisdom." In tales throughout the world—Innana's seven-staged descent into Hades, the seven rungs of the ladder to Heaven, the seven years of bounty and then famine in biblical Egypt, the seven loaves in Gilgamesh—all pertain to the steps of an inner journey, of psycho-spiritual death and then rebirth. See Henderson's *Wisdom of the Serpent*, pp. 41, 71–73.

EPILOGUE

1 Campbell, *The Hero with a Thousand Faces,* p. 217.
2 John G. Neihardt, *Black Elk Speaks* (New York: Washington Square Press, 1959), p. 41.

ACKNOWLEDGMENTS

ONE MORNING, when I was barely more than three years old, my sister took my hand with urgency and led me downstairs, sat me in front of our large Zenith black-and-white television. Planted, I watched the screen crackle alive—another episode of the "Modern Farmer"—a constant of early Saturday morning television in the fifties, and I waited while she turned the volume up so that no one could hear what she was about to confide. "When Mozart was only three years old," she said with a single-minded earnest that only a child could muster, "he composed his first minuet." She let that sink into my loyal but bewildered ears. "When he was four, he played concerts throughout the world!" "Now, I don't know, but I just don't think he learned how to do that in just four years. I think he learned it *before*." She searched my eyes for a moment, then arose and left.

The unexpected surrounds us. I have now heard many fantastic stories. In truth, I believe it is the little events that are so special: a moment of emotional surrender at the theater; the improbable rebound of a child after a colossal fall; a crescent moon against the dark purple of an early evening sky; the smell of wild sage in the morning. In all its beatific and frightful guises, the unexpected reminds us of the boundless magnificence of this life, and I feel privileged to have been able to enter its world.

Writing any book requires a prolonged meditation on the nature of its subject. As is true of such a total engagement, an author is visited, time and again, by the very themes he or she endeavors to render. During the nearly three years of this book's creation, the unexpected has come in many forms. (In truth, it sometimes felt as though a benign, yet demented relative had come to visit, and stayed a bit too long.)

This journey has brought incalculable delights and dramatic terrors, wonderful opportunities and formidable challenges. Clearly, the completion of a book on the unexpected was going to require nothing less than traversing its labyrinth firsthand. Indeed, I began to believe that some greater force or intelligence was actually *prohibiting* a dispassionate discourse from a safe distance, as if that era, that age of cool intellectual analysis concerning the most important moments of our lives, was over.

All creative endeavors require the indulgence, sacrifice, and goodwill of others. This is especially true of a project on the unexpected. There are many dear friends and family who have supported this work and without whom, its completion would have been impossible. My wife, Lucinda, horticultural artiste extraordinaire, who has persevered with me through the unanticipated peaks and valleys of this project and who continued to nurture the seeds of our family. Wayne Muller, for the gift of his insight and steadfast devotion to our lifelong friendship in its many forms. My indebtedness to my crew of para-editors: Devi Records, a superlative therapist and structural editor, who responded to incalculable editions with clarity and humor; poet and therapist Jon Eisman for his analyses on the run; and Wendy Heckler, muse incarnate, for her unswerving encouragement and enthusiasm. My appreciation to my agent and friend, Loretta Barrett, who under extreme circumstances, demonstrated her unsurpassed skill and allegiance through the course of this work, and to Jane Isay, who remains one of the last, great, writer's editors, for her loyalty. The late Donald Sandner, M.D., whose clinical supervision was unsurpassed and whose Laughing Buddha–mentorship I sorely miss. Kathryn Fisher, who, long ago, taught me how to write the "first word."

Once again, my gratitude extends to larger professional communities for supporting my endeavors and encouraging my meanderings. To my colleagues and students at the Hakomi Institute worldwide, for their goodwill and flexibility, and to my friends at JFK University for the same. Douglas and Rachel Anderson who suffered the ramblings, odd enthusiasms, and non sequiturs that writers are prone to, and the McDougals and Marcus-Willers for their new friendship. To Fred and the staff at Browser Books, one of San Francisco's consummate independent bookstores, for allowing my endless loitering, and finally, to Sheila, Anita, and Bob at the Breakaway Café, one of the true American breakfast nooks, for their fresh fruit and ribald morning humor.

INDEX